POEMS
BY
JOHN ROLLIN RIDGE
with his
OTHER POEMS

Edited by
Wanda C. Patterson and J. B. Tate
New edition co-edited by W. Jeff Bishop
Georgia Chapter National Trail of Tears Association
Newnan, Georgia

Boll Weevil Press
2017

Ridge, John Rollin, 1827–1867
    Poems.
    Edited by Wanda C. Patterson and J. B. Tate, 2005. New edition co-edited by W. Jeff Bishop, 2017. Originally published by Edward Bosque & Co., San Francisco, 1868.
    1. Cherokee Indians — Poetry. I. Ridge, John Rollin. II. Title.
    PS2699 .R75   2017   811.08
    ISBN:0988956810

    Book designed by Dale Lyles.
    Fonts: editorial material, Century Schoolbook; replica text, Century modern TT

EDITORS' PREFACE.

The Georgia Chapter of the National Trail of Tears Association is pleased to present this reprinting of *POEMS* by Cherokee author John Rollin Ridge. The original volume was published posthumously by his wife Elizabeth Wilson Ridge in 1868 and was recently discovered in the library of the Etowah Valley Historical Society, Cartersville, Georgia. It is our desire that the reissue of this collection of poems from the many written by Ridge will not only stand alone as an object of interest, but will also introduce John Rollin Ridge to an audience of historians, literary scholars, and most particularly the legion of individuals involved in exploring the history of the Cherokee people and the Trail of Tears.

The story of John Rollin Ridge provides a window into the lives of Cherokees in what was to become Oklahoma Territory *after* the tragedy of the Trail of Tears. Volumes have been written concerning the events leading up to the Trail and the horrific journey itself. However, most scholars conclude their telling of the Cherokee story when the survivors reach their destination. What is not widely detailed is that decades of strife marred life among the various factions of Cherokees, as their leaders struggled over who would control the government and treasury of a fledgling nation in a new land. John Rollin Ridge grew to manhood in the midst of that struggle and, as Ridge states in an 1849 letter, events in that struggle "darkened my mind with an eternal shadow."

John Rollin Ridge was born on March 19, 1827, into a prominent Cherokee family in the pre-Removal Cherokee Nation. His grandfather, Major Ridge, was a highly regarded Cherokee leader, a prosperous businessman and land owner on what is now the location of Chieftains Museum, Rome, Georgia. Running Waters, the 419-acre farm of Rollin's successful attorney father, John Ridge, was located on the Oostanaula River, near present-day Rome. His mother, Sarah Bird Northrup Ridge, was the daughter of a respected Connecticut family, whom John met while he was enrolled in a foreign missions school in Cornwall, Connecticut. The marriage between a white girl and an Indian was controversial among the residents of Cornwall; however, Sarah was welcomed into her new Cherokee family.

The John Ridge family recognized the value of education and built a schoolhouse on their property, where the Ridge family children were instructed by a Massachusetts missionary, Miss Sophia Sawyer. Among the subjects of study were the "three Rs," as well as history, geography, English literature, and the Bible. The Ridge family moved west when Rollin was ten; and the Ridges again provided a schoolhouse for Miss Sawyer, who continued to teach the Ridge children. An excellent student, Rollin's education continued in both Arkansas and Massachusetts, studying Latin, Greek, ancient history and geography, and classical literature. His concluded his education in the study of the law.

What appeared to be a privileged life for young Rollin was interrupted at age 10 by events beyond his control, the consequences of which would leave an indelible stamp on every chapter of his life. The Cherokee Nation was subjected to unrelenting pressure by the national government of President Andrew Jackson and the state of Georgia to give up the Cherokee homeland in exchange for unknown land west of the Mississippi. Major Ridge and John Ridge joined Chief John Ross and other Cherokee leaders in resisting emigration, repeatedly sending delegations to Washington to plead the Cherokee case.

When the state of Georgia passed punitive laws designed to drive the Cherokees out, and the federal government ignored a Supreme Court ruling in the Cherokees' favor, the Ridges and certain other tribal leaders abandoned what they viewed as a hopeless struggle to reverse the tide which had obviously turned against them. Thus, the Cherokee Nation divided into the treaty party, which supported a removal treaty, and the Ross faction, which backed Chief John Ross's continued efforts to resist removal.

Major Ridge, John Ridge, and CHEROKEE PHOENIX editor Elias Boudinot were among 20 Cherokees who signed the Treaty of New Echota, agreeing to sell Cherokee land in exchange for money and land in the West. In 1836 the treaty was ratified by a one-vote margin in the Senate, despite the fact that the vast majority of Cherokees opposed the treaty. Although the actions of the treaty party reflected what they believed to be in the best interests of the Cherokees, their signatures on the Treaty were equivalent to a death sentence, since an 1829 Cherokee law ordered death for anyone who sold Cherokee land without majority approval.

While the Ross party continued to fight removal through diplomatic means, the Ridges and other treaty families sold their land and business enterprises and moved to the West by the end of 1837. There they settled among Cherokees who had emigrated a number of years earlier, accepting their existing government and laws. The Ridge family properties were located at Honey Creek near the Missouri border of Cherokee land.

When the Ross party's resistance to the removal was ultimately defeated, government troops rounded up the remaining Cherokees, many of them without the most basic supplies, and forced their removal to the West during late 1838 and early 1839. Over 4,000 Cherokees, mostly children and the elderly, died on the Trail of Tears, suffering disease, freezing weather, and all manner of depredations as they struggled over nine hundred frozen miles to reach Cherokee Territory. Notable among the dead was Chief Ross's wife, Quatie, as well as large numbers of deceased Cherokees who were buried in unmarked graves along the trail. Needless to say, the survivors were angry and resentful and ultimately laid the blame for their troubles at the feet of the Ridges and other signers, despite the f act that the removal was instigated by the U.S. government, not the treaty party.

Immediate conflict arose in the new Cherokee Nation among the various factions, regarding which government would be in charge, that of Chief John Ross or the previously established government of the early settlers. Reaching an impasse, a group of Ross supporters broke the stalemate by assassinating three signers of the Treaty of New Echota. Major Ridge, John Ridge, and Elias Boudinot were ambushed and killed. John Ridge's executioners broke into his home and stabbed him 26 times, as his horrified wife and children helplessly looked on. John Rollin Ridge, a 12-year-old witness, spent the rest of his life torn between avenging his father's death or devoting himself to restoring the fortune and reputation of the Ridge family name.

Fearing for her family's safety, Sarah Ridge moved her children to Fayetteville, Arkansas. Ensuing conflicts over the Ridge property and money due from the Treaty settlement resulted in financial difficulties which plagued the Ridge family for years. Young Rollin completed his education in Arkansas, and there he married a lovely white girl, Elizabeth Wilson. The couple settled at Honey Creek in the Cherokee Nation, where they farmed and welcomed a daughter, Alice.

In 1850 Rollin joined the California gold rush, having fled the Cherokee Nation after shooting a neighbor in a quarrel over a horse. Many believed the incident was instigated by a Ross supporter, who pressed the quarrel in an effort to get rid of Rollin, whose influence might diminish Ross's power. Claiming self-defense, but fearing that he would not get a fair trial, Rollin joined a westward bound wagon train, determined to earn his fortune in the California gold fields before sending for his young family.

Rollin, his brother Aenias, and a slave risked their lives repeatedly during their perilous three-month journey to California. They ran out of money and supplies, ditched or sold most of their equipment and animals, and faced long stretches without food or water while crossing mountains and deserts. Then, to their great disappointment, they discovered that mining was an expensive, labor-intensive occupation which depended more on luck than hard work; and few men struck it rich. After several months of back-breaking work, Rollin and company gave up on instant riches and looked for jobs which offered more dependable compensation.

When Ridge arrived in Sacramento in 1850, he put his education to work instead of his pick axe, securing his first newspaper job as a correspondent for a New Orleans newspaper, *TRUE DELTA*. He wrote articles, sold papers and books, and began to sell an occasional poem for publication. He had found his calling as a journalist.

During the next 16 years, Ridge worked for a series of California newspapers, supplementing his income with positions in local government, and eventually worked himself up to editor and part owner of eight different papers. His income was then sufficient to send for his wife and daughter, purchase land, and build a house for his little family.

In addition to his work as a journalist and poet, Ridge's reputation, if not his fortune was made with the publication of THE LIFE AND ADVENTURES OF JOAQUIN MURIETA, THE CELEBRATED CALIFORNIA BANDIT. He published the novel under the pseudonym "Yellow Bird," the name given to him as a child by his grandfather, Major Ridge. However, his true identity was soon made public. The popularity of the book was enhanced by the fact that it was written by a dashing, accomplished young Cherokee, as well as by the controversy which arose over the authenticity of the events Ridge related as carefully researched fact in his book.

The story was based on newspaper accounts of the exploits of an actual Mexican bandit, who established quite a colorful reputation in California. He was feared by some, and revered by others as a kind of Robin Hood, taking what he could from those who had wronged him. The book enjoyed wide readership and was variously plagiarized in numerous periodicals. Amazingly, historians of the period took Ridge's colorful account for fact and included information from Ridge's story in early histories of California.

John Rollin Ridge is credited with several "firsts," as a result of the publication of JOAQUIN MURIETA in 1854. The book was the first novel published in California. It was also the first novel written by a Native American. Since the success of Ridge's book spawned a thriving nineteenth-century industry in novels about rugged heroes and villains of the old West, he has been called the father of the "dime novel."

Ridge's respect as a poet is underlined by the number of public occasions for which he was asked to compose special poems. For example, he wrote a remarkable poem to commemorate the laying of the transatlantic cable between the U.S. and Britain in 1858. As did many other American cities, the town of Marysville, where Ridge was editor of the DAILY NA-

TIONAL DEMOCRAT, hosted a brilliant celebration of the cable, featuring music and speeches. The centerpiece of the event was the striking figure of John Rollin Ridge, eloquently reading "Poem on the Atlantic Cable." According to James W. Parins' *JOHN ROLLIN RIDGE—HIS LIFE AND WORK*, "the crowd broke into enthusiastic applause" as the poem ended.[1] In 100 lines, Ridge traced the history of communication from primitive "skin-clad messengers" to the scientific feats of Ben Franklin and Samuel Morse, all leading up to the crowning achievement of the cable, which would link all mankind and create universal peace!

In part, Ridge's popularity as a poet and public speaker could be attributed to the fact that a number of his verses, such as "Mount Shasta," extolled the beauty and majesty of California. Ridge's artistry as a poet rested in his evocative descriptions of scene and atmosphere. His poems showcased the breadth of his education through the many allusions to classical literature and ancient history which he employed. For those less erudite, his numerous love poems were appealing. Several of Ridge's poems are intensely patriotic, a somewhat amazing point, considering the hardships suffered by Native peoples at the hands of the United States government. He read his compositions at various Fourth of July celebrations.

Ridge's career as a journalist was often punctuated with public wars of words, trading insults with the editors of competing newspapers. On a number of occasions these battles extended beyond the printed page and resulted in challenges to duel. Possibly because of Ridge's reputation as a "crack" shot, his opponents were usually the first to blink, thus avoiding bloodshed. During one such dispute, Ridge thoroughly trashed his counterpart with a walking stick!

Ridge was intensely interested in the politics of the day and spoke out on a wide range of issues. Through his editorials, he became a powerful force in support of Stephen A. Douglas, who opposed Abraham Lincoln in the 1860 Presidential election, which hinged primarily on the slavery question. As a slave owner, Ridge naturally supported popular sovereignty and raged against

---

[1] p. 142

what he considered to be Lincoln's radical policies.

Ridge continued his anti-Lincoln diatribes at the San Francisco *EVENING JOURNAL*, where he garnered accolades, even from the editor of a competing paper. Parins' biography of Ridge contains the following description of Ridge's skill as a journalist: "Our contemporary, the Evening Journal, is fortunate in having secured the editorial cooperation of John R. Ridge. This gentleman has, as editor of the National Democrat, at Marysville, shown himself to be a vigorous writer and an uncompromising Union man. His editorial articles are always terse, perspicuous, free from prejudice and clothed in elegant English. Mr. Ridge is more fortunate than some of the fraternity, inasmuch as he is a poet of no mean pretensions."[2]

In 1864 Ridge bought an interest in the daily paper, the Grass Valley *NATIONAL*, and served as its editor. It was in the *NATIONAL* that he abandoned his pro-Union stance and came out solidly in support of the Confederacy. Throughout his exile in California, Ridge had always kept abreast of events in the Cherokee Nation, where the old Ridge-Ross rivalries still simmered. The Civil War split the Nation along factional lines, with the Ridge faction supporting the Confederacy, while the Ross party allied with the Union. In fact, Ridge's cousin, Stand Watie, brother of Elias Boudinot, became a brigadier general in the Confederate Army and was the last officer to surrender his command.

When the Civil War ended, each Indian tribe was required to negotiate a new treaty with the federal government. Although Ridge had not set foot in the Cherokee Nation since he departed for California in 1850, he was invited to represent the Nation as part of the Southern delegation of Cherokee who went to Washington in 1866 to negotiate on behalf of the Cherokees who had supported the Confederacy. Although attempts were made to divide the land and treasury of the Cherokee Nation between the pro-Union Ross party and the Southern Cherokees, cooler heads prevailed, and the Cherokees remained a single Nation. Interestingly, the Southern delegation included the "third generation" of some of the most prominent old

---

[2] pp. 184-85

Cherokee families: the Ridges, the Boudinots, the Waties, and the Adairs.

John Rollin Ridge died in 1867 at the age of 40 of a condition called "brain fever," probably the result of a stroke. He was buried in the Ridge family plot in Grass Valley, California. Even rival newspapers praised him in obituaries.

Elizabeth Wilson Ridge published a collection of her husband's poetry in 1868. It is a faithful reproduction of that volume that the Georgia Chapter of the National Trail of Tears Association takes pride in offering as our contribution to the continuing legacy of the Ridge family and a tribute to the life and accomplishments of a remarkable son of the Cherokee Nation.

Wanda C. Patterson, Editor

In 1933 the Native Sons of the Golden West honored the memory of John Rollin Ridge by placing a stone marker in the Ridge family plot in Greenwood Cemetery at Grass Valley, California. The monument is inscribed as follows:

"John Rollin Ridge—California poet, Author of "Mount Shasta" and Other Poems. Born March 19, 1827, in Cherokee Nation, near what is now Rome, Georgia. Died in Grass Valley, October 5, 1867. In Grateful Memory."
Photo courtesy of Robin Soule, California.

Elizabeth Wilson Ridge, wife of John Rollin Ridge.
Photo courtesy of Paul Ridenour.

John Rollin Ridge.
Photo courtesy of Paul Ridenour.

Sarah Northrup Ridge, mother of John Rollin Ridge.
Photo courtesy of Paul Ridenour.

John Rollin Ridge.
Picture from original POEMS book.

John Rollin Ridge and daughter Alice Bird.
Photo courtesy of Paul Ridenour.

Southern delegation of Cherokees, appointed to negotiate new treaty with U.S. in 1866 (l to r): John Rollin Ridge, Saladin Watie, Richard Fields, Elias Cornelius Boudinot, William Penn Adair. (not pictured: Stand Watie, Joseph A. Scales).
Photo courtesy of the Archives and Manuscript Division of the Oklahoma Historical Society.

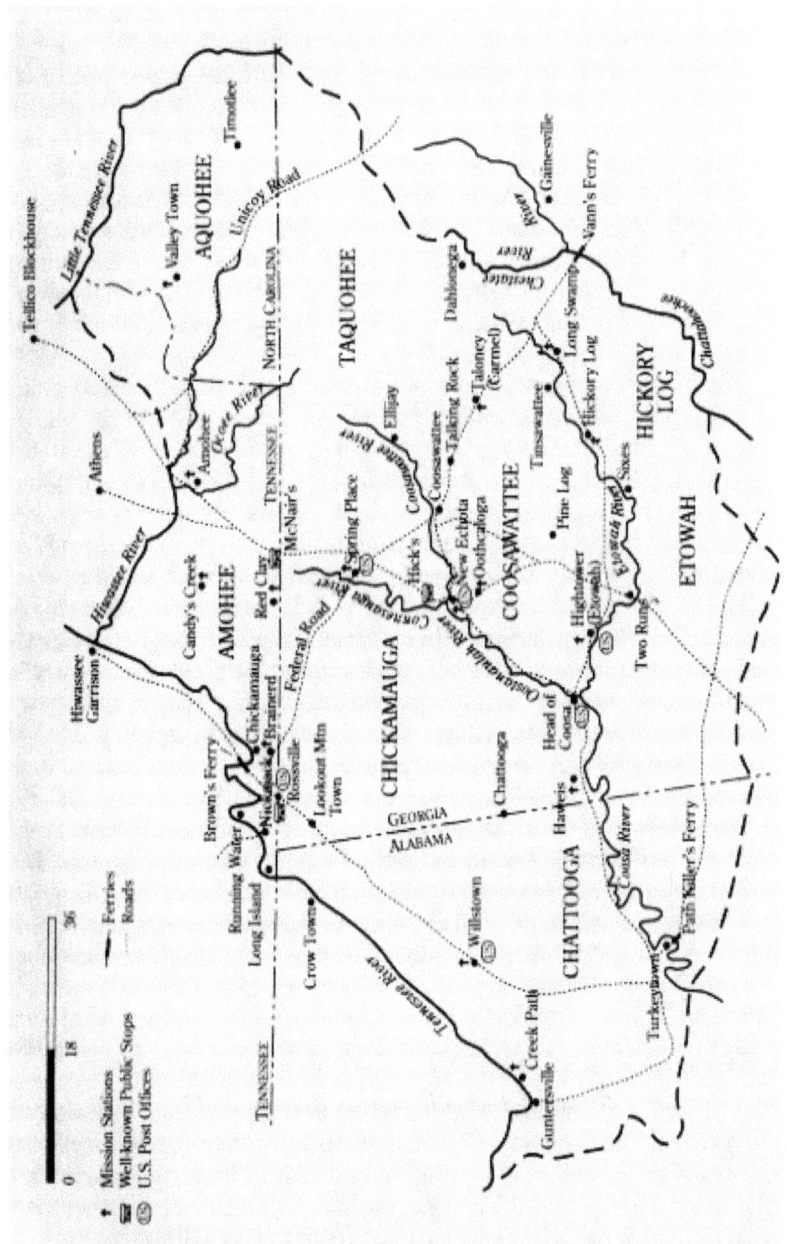

Cherokee Nation 1825

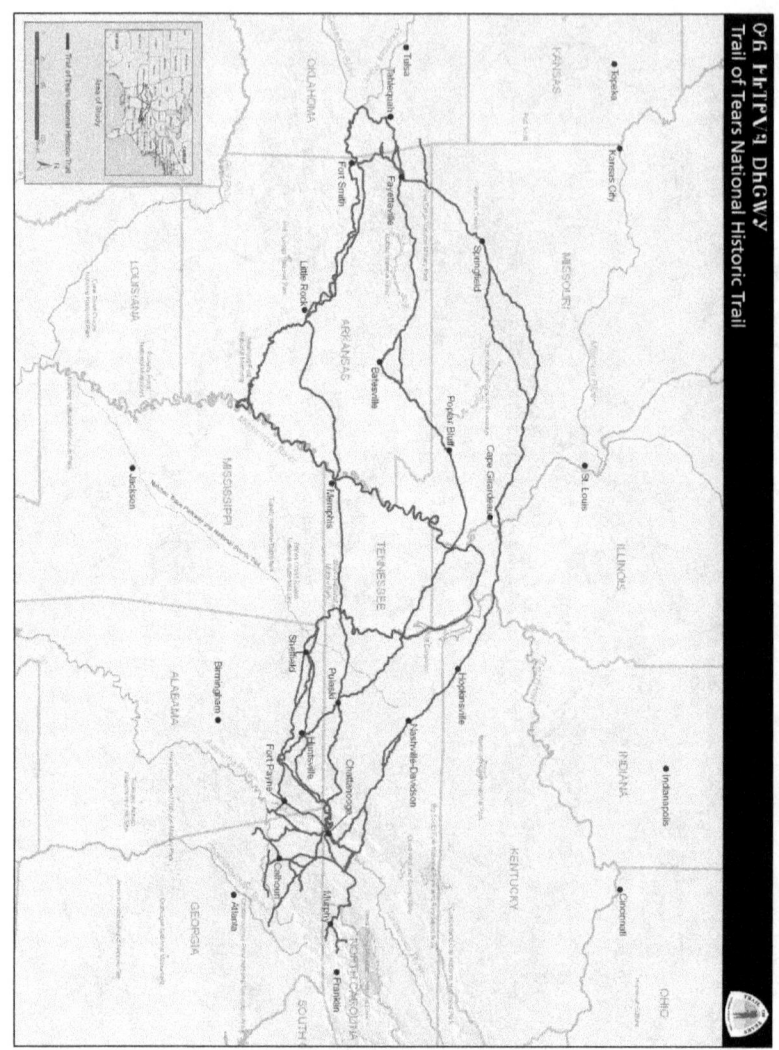

Trail of Tears Removal Routes 1837

ACKNOWLEDGEMENTS

GA TOTA is enormously grateful to the remarkable research of Dr. James W. Parins, author of *JOHN ROLLIN RIDGE—HIS LIFE AND WORK*, which served as a guide for this Preface. For scholars of Cherokee history, Parins' book is a veritable goldmine of information. The book is available through the University of Nebraska Press (www.nebraskapress.unl.edu) Dr. Parins has also written *ELIAS CORNELIUS BOUDINOT*, a biography of Elisa Boudinot's eldest son. Parins is professor of English and director of the American Native Press Archives at the University of Arkansas at Little Rock.

The generosity of the Etowah Valley Historical Society, Bartow County, Georgia, is most appreciated for their having loaned their treasured volume of *POEMS* by J.R. Ridge for this reprinting. Special thanks go to Michael Garland for his valuable counsel in sharing his knowledge of procedures for reprints.

Many thanks to Carla S. Gossett of Lite Brite Publishing Solutions, Smyrna, Georgia for her creative input and publishing expertise in the first reprint of *POEMS* in 2005.

Thanks go to Mr. and Mrs. Paul Ridenour, Garland, Texas, for sharing photos and insights from their website regarding their ancestors, the Ridges.

POEMS.

Entered according to Act of Congress, in the year 1868, by
Mrs. JOHN R. RIDGE,
In the Clerk's Office of the District Court of the United
States for the District of California.
EDWARD BOSQUE CO., PRINTERS,
517 Clay Street, San Francisco.

PREFACE.

Most of the poems in this little volume are the productions of boyhood; very few of them were written after the author had reached the age of twenty. Like other men of his temperament, Mr. Ridge lost in the excitement of political life his youthful ambition for literary fame; consequently, many of his latest and best poems have been lost. Some that are embodied here, however, have elicited high praise from the Pacific and Eastern press. The severe critic may think that it had been better taste, perhaps, to have omitted some which have here been preserved—and he may be correct; but, they who have treasured the worn-out shoe and useless, threadbare garment of one who has gone to return no more, will not be harsh in their judgment of our taste.

The propriety of prefacing this book with a biographical sketch of the author has been suggested to us. Such a sketch must necessarily be short. To go into the details of a life fraught with many stirring incidents, would require time; and, as we have not the requisite time at our command, we propose to give Mr. Ridge's own brief account of his parentage, and that dark misfortune of his childhood which cast a shadow over his whole life, as we find it in a letter written by him to a friend in 1849— only a few months before he came to California. As, his career on this coast, in connection with political and literary journalism, is familiar to all readers, we will add nothing to this letter.

"I was born in the Cherokee Nation, East of the Mississippi River, on the 19th of March, 1827. My earliest recollections are of such things as are pleasing to childhood, the fondness of a kind father, and smiles of an affectionate mother. My father, the late John Ridge, as you know, was one of the Chiefs of his tribe, and son of the warrior and orator distinguished in Cherokee Councils and battles, who was known amongst the whites as Major Ridge, and amongst his own people as Ka-nun-ta-cla-ge. My father grew up till he was some twelve or fifteen years of age, as any untutored Indian, and he used well to remember the time when his greatest delight was to strip himself of his Indian costume, and with aboriginal cane-gig in hand, while away the long summer days in wading up and down creeks in search of crawfish.

"At the age which I have mentioned above, a missionary station sprang into existence, and Major Ridge sent his son John, who could not speak word of English, to school at this station, placing him under the instruction of a venerable Missionary named Gambol. Here he learned rapidly, and in the course of a year acquired a sufficient knowledge of the white man's language to speak it quite fluently.

"Major Ridge had now become fully impressed with the importance of civilization He had built him a log-cabin, in imitation of the border-whites and opened him a farm. The Missionary, Gambol, told him of an institution built up in a distant land expressly for the education of Indian youths (Cornwall, Connecticut), and here he concluded to send his son. After hearing some stern advice from his father, with respect to the manner to which lie should conduct himself amongst the 'pale-faces,' he departed for the Cornwall School in charge of a friendly Missionary. He remained there until his education was completed. During his attendance at this institution, he fell in love with a young white girl of the place, daughter of Mr. Northrup. His love was reciprocated. He returned home to his father, gained his consent, though with much difficulty (for the old Major wished him to marry a chief's daughter amongst his own people), went lack again to Cornwall, and shortly brought his "pale-faced" bride to the wild country of the Cherokees. In due course of time, I, John Rollin, came into the world. I was called by my grandfather 'Chees-quat-a-law-ny,' which, interpreted, means 'Yellow Bird.' Thus you have a knowledge of my parentage and how it happened that I am an Indian.

"Things had now changed with the Cherokees, They had a written Constitution and laws. They had legislative halls, houses and farms, courts, and juries. The general mass, it is true, were ignorant, but happy under the administration of a few simple, just, and wholesome laws. Major Ridge had become wealthy by trading with the whites and by prudent management. He had built an elegant house on the banks of the 'Oos-te-nar-ly River,' on which now stands the thriving town of Rome, Georgia. Many a time in my buoyant boyhood have I strayed along its summer-shaded shores and glided in the light canoe over its swiftly-rolling bosom, and beneath its over-hanging willows. Alas for the beautiful scene! The Indian's form haunts it no more!

"My father's residence was a few miles east of the 'Qos-te-narly.' I remember it well. A large two-storied house, on a high hill crowned with a fine grove of oak and hickory, a large, clear spring at the foot of the hill, and an extensive farm stretching away down into the valley, with a fine orchard on the left. On another hill some two hundred yards distant, stood the schoolhouse, built at my father's expense, for the use of a Missionary, Miss Sophia Sawyer, who made her home with our family and taught my father's children and all who chose to come for her instruction. I went to this school until I was ten years of age— which was in 1837. Then another change had come over the Cherokee Nation. A demon-spell had fallen upon it. The white man had become covetous of the soil. The unhappy Indian was driven from his house—not one, but thousand—and the white man's ploughshare turned up the acres which he had called his own. Wherever the Indian built his cabin, and planted his corn, there was the spot which the white man craved. Convicted on suspicion, they were sentenced to death by laws whose authority they could not acknowledge, and hanged on the white man's gallows. Oppression became intolerable, and forced by extreme necessity, they at last gave up their homes, yielded their beloved country to the rapacity of the Georgians, and wended their way in silence and in sorrow to the forests of the far west. In 1837, my father moved his family to his new home, he built his houses and opened his farm; gave encouragement to the rising neighborhood, and fed many a hungry and naked Indian whom oppression had prostrated, to the dust. A second time he built a schoolhouse, and Miss Sawyer again instructed his own children and the children of his neighbors. Two years culled away in quietude but the Spring of 1839 brought in a terrible train of events. Parties had arisen in the Nation. The removal West had fomented discontents of the darkest and deadliest nature. The ignorant Indians, unable to vent their rage on the whites, turned their wrath towards their own chiefs, and chose to hold them responsible for what had happened. John Ross made use of these prejudices to establish his own power. He held a secret council and plotted the death of my father and grandfather, and Boudinot, and others, who were friendly to the interests of these men. John Ridge was at this time the most powerful man in the Nation, and it was necessary for Ross, in order to realize his ambitious scheme for ruling the whole Nation, not only to put the Ridges out of the way, but those who most prominently supported them, lest they might cause trouble afterwards. These bloody deeds were perpetrated under circumstances of peculiar aggravation. On the morning of the 22nd of June, 1839, about day-break, our family was aroused from sleep by a violent noise. The doors were broken down, and the house was full of armed men. I saw my father in the hands of assassins. He endeavored so speak to them, but they shouted and drowned his voice for they were instructed not to listen so him for a moment for fear they would be persuaded not to kill him. They dragged him into the yard, and prepared to murder him. Two men held him by the arms, and others by the body, while another stabbed him deliberately with a dirk twenty-nine times. My mother rushed out to the door, but they pushed her back with their guns into the house, and prevented her egress until their act was finished, when they left the place quietly. My father fell to earth but did not immediately expire. My mother ran out to him. He raised himself on his elbow and tried to speak, but the blood flowed into his mouth and prevented him. In a few moments more he died, without speaking that last word which he wished to say. Then succeeded a scene of agony the sight of which might make one regret that the human race had ever been created. It has darkened my mind with an eternal shadow. In a room prepared for the purpose, lay pale in death the man whose voice had been listened to with awe and admiration in the councils of his Nation, and whose fame had passed to the remotest of the United States, the blood oozing through his winding sheet, and falling drop by drop on the floor. By his side sat my mother, with hands clasped, and its speechless agony— she who had given him her heart in the days of her youth and beauty, left the home of her parents, and followed the husband of her choice to a wild and distant land. And bending over him was his own afflicted mother, with her long, white hair flung loose over her shoulders. and bosom, crying to the Great Spirit to sustain her in that dreadful hour. And in addition to all these, the wife, the mother and the little children, who scarcely knew their loss, were the dark faces of those who had been the murdered man's friends, and, possibly, some who had been privy to the assassination, who had come to smile over the scene.

"There was yet another blow to be dealt. Major Ridge had started on a journey the day before to Van Buren, a town on the Arkansas River, in the State of Arkansas. He was traveling down what was called the Line Road, its the direction of Evansville. A runner was sent with all possible speed to inform him of what had happened. The runner returned with the news that Major Ridge himself was killed. It is useless to lengthen description. It would fall short far short of the theme.

"These events happened when I was twelve years old. Great excitement existed in the Nation, and my mother thinking her children unsafe in the country of their father's murders, and unwilling to remain longer where all that she saw reminded her of her dreadful bereavement, removed to the State of Arkansas, and settled in the town of Fayetteville. In that place I went to school till I was fourteen years of age, when my mother sent me to New England to finish my education. There is was that I became acquainted with you, and you know all about my history during my attendance at the Great Barrington School as well as I do myself. Owing to the rigor of the climate my health failed me about the time I was ready to enter college, and I returned to my mother in Arkansas. Here I read Latin and Greek, and pursued my studies with the Rev. Cephas Washbourne (who had formerly been a Missionary in the Cherokee Nation) till the summer of 1845 when the difficulties which had existed in the Nation ever since my father's death, more or less, had drawn to a crisis"...[3]

"Thus have I briefly and hurriedly complied with your request, and given you a sketch of my life. I shall not return to the Nation now until circumstances are materially changed. I shall cast my fortunes for some years with the whites. I am twenty-three years old, married, and have an infant daughter. I will still devote my life to my people, though not amongst them, and before I die, I hope to see the Cherokee Nation, in conjunction, with the Choctaws, admitted into the Confederacy of the United States."

---

[3] Here follows a history of Cherokee affairs, embracing the years 1845 and '46, and Mr. Ridge's connection therewith, which we think proper to omit.

Table of Contents.

MOUNT SHASTA...11
THE ATLANTIC CABLE. 13
FAITH..16
HUMBOLDT RIVER. 17
TO A YOUNG LADY. 19
TO A STAR SEEN AT TWILIGHT....................................20
REMEMBRANCE OF A SUMMER'S NIGHT....................22
TO LIZZIE. 26
THE FORGIVEN DEAD..28
TO A MOCKING BIRD SINGING IN A TREE. 29
MARY, QUEEN OF SCOTS. 30
A CHEROKEE LOVE SONG. 31
DEDICATION FOR AN ALBUM. 32
THE RAINY SEASON IN CALIFORNIA. 33
THE HARP OF BROKEN STRINGS. 36
OCTOBER HILLS. 38
THE MAID OF THE MOUNTAINS...................................39
ON YUBA CITY..40
OF HER I LOVE...42
TO THE BEAUTIFUL...43
A NIGHT SCENE. 44
ODE TO THE NATIONAL FLAG......................................46
To C——. 48
ROSA DUNN...49
FALSE, BUT BEAUTIFUL. 50
TO L—— ON RECEIVING HER PORTRAIT...................50
THE STOLEN WHITE GIRL. 52
A JUNE MORNING. 53
THE SABBATH BELLS. 54
POEM..56
ERINNA. 60
LINES ON A HUMMING BIRD 62
CALIFORNIA. 63
MY LOST LOVE. 67
POEM. 68
THE "SINGING SPIRIT." 72

DO I LOVE THEE?	73
A SCENE ALONG THE RIO DE LAS PLUMAS.	75
THE STILL SMALL VOICE.	78
EYES.	79
POEM.	81
THE ARKANSAW ROOT DOCTOR.	91
THE MAIDEN'S FORTUNE.	95
RANDOM THOUGHTS OF HER.	97
OTHER POEMS.	99
TO A****.	101
FAR IN A LONELY WOOD.	101
THE STILL SMALL VOICE.	103
THE HUMBOLDT DESERT.	105
SONG— SWEET INDIAN MAID.	107

MOUNT SHASTA.

BEHOLD the dread Mt. Shasta, where it stands
Imperial midst the lesser heights, and, like
Some mighty unimpassioned mind, companionless
And cold. The storms of Heaven may beat in wrath
Against it, but it stands in unpolluted
Grandeur still ; and from the rolling mists upheaves
Its tower of pride e'en purer than before.
The wintry showers and white-winged tempests leave
Their frozen tributes on its brow, and it
Doth make of them an everlasting crown.
Thus doth it, day by day and age by age,
Defy each stroke of time still rising highest
Into Heaven!

Aspiring to the eagle's cloudless height,
No human foot has stained its snowy side;
No human breath has dimmed the icy mirror which
It holds unto the moon and stars and sov'reign sun.
We may not grow familiar with the secrets
Of its hoary top, whereon the Genius
Of that mountain builds his glorious throne!
Far lifted in the boundless blue, he doth
Encircle, with his gaze supreme, the broad
Dominions of the West, which lie beneath
His feet, in pictures of sublime repose
No artist ever drew. He sees the tall
Gigantic hills arise in silentness
And peace, and in the long review of distance
Range themselves in order grand. He sees the sunlight
Play upon the golden streams which through the valleys
Glide. He hears the music of the great and solemn sea,
And overlooks the huge old western wall
To view the birth-place of undying Melody!

Itself all light, save when some loftiest cloud
Doth for a while embrace its cold forbidding
Form, that monarch mountain casts its mighty
Shadow down upon the crownless peaks below,
That, like inferior minds to some great
Spirit, stand in strong contrasted littleness!
All through the long and Summery months of our
Most tranquil year, it points its icy shaft
On high, to catch the dazzling beams that fall
In showers of splendor round that crystal cone,
And roll in floods of far magnificence
Away from that lone, vast Reflector in
The dome of Heaven
Still watchful of the fertile
Vale and undulating plains below, the grass
Grows greener. In its shade, and sweeter bloom
The flowers. Strong purifier! From its snowy
Side the breezes cool are wafted to the "peaceful
Homes of men," who shelter at its feet, and love
To gaze upon its honored form, aye standing
There the guarantee of health and happiness.
Well might it win communities so blest
To loftier feelings and to nobler thoughts—
The great material symbol of eternal
Things! And well I ween in after years, how
In the middle of his furrowed track the plowman
In some sultry hour will pause, and wiping
From his brow the dusty, with reverence
Gaze upon that hoary peak. The herdsman
Oft will rein his charger in the plain, and drink
Into his inmost soul the calm sublimity;
And little childen, playing on the green, shall
Cease their sport, and, turning to that mountain
Old, shall of their mother ask: "Who made it?"
And she shall answer, — "GOD!"

And well this Golden State shall thrive, if like
Its own Mt. Shasta, Sovereign Law shall lift
Itself in purer atmosphere—so high
That human feeling, human passion at its base
Shall lie subdued; e'en pity's tears shall on
Its summit freeze; to warm it e'en the sunlight
Of deep sympathy shall fail:
Its pure administration shall be like
The snow immaculate upon that mountain's brow!

THE ATLANTIC CABLE.

Let Earth be glad! for that great work is done,
Which makes, at last; the Old and New World one!
Let all mankind rejoice! for time nor space
Shall check the progress of the human race!
Though Nature heaved the Continents apart,
She cast in one great mould the human heart;
She framed on one great plan the human mind
And gave man speech to link him to his kind;
So that, though plains and mountains intervene,
Or oceans, broad and stormy, roll between
If there but be a courier for the thought—
Swift-winged or slow—the land and seas are nought,
And man is nearer to his brother brought.

First, ere the dawn of letters was, or burst
The light of science on the world, men, nurs't
In distant solitudes apart, did send,
Their skin-clad heralds forth to thread the woods,
Scale mountain-peaks, or swim the sudden floods,
And bear their messages of peace or war.

Next, beasts were tamed to drag the rolling car,
Or speed the mounted rider on his track;
And then came, too, the vessels, oar-propelled,
Which fled the ocean, as the clouds grew black,
And safe near shore their prudent courses held.
Next came the winged ships, which, brave and free,
Did skim the bosom of the bounding sea;
And dared the storms and darkness in their flight,
Yet drifted far before the winds and night;
Or lay within the dead calm's grasp of might.
Then, sea-divided nations nearer came,
Stood face to face, spake each the other's name,
In friendship grew, and learned the truth sublime,
That Man is Man in every age and clime
They nearer were by months and years—but space
Must still be shortened in Improvement's race,
And steam came next to wake the world from sleep,
And launch her black-plumed warriors of the deep;
The which, in calm or storm, rode onward still,
And braved the raging elements at will.
Then distance, which from calms' and storms' delays
Grew into months, was shortened into days,
And Science' self declared her wildest dream
Reached not beyond this miracle of steam!
But steam hath not the lightning's wondrous power,
Though, Titan-like, mid Science' sons it tower
And wrestle with the ocean in his wrath,
And sweep the wild waves foaming from its path.
A mightier monarch is that subtler thing;
Which gives to human thought a thought-swift wing;
Which speaks in thunder like a God,
Or humbly stoops to kiss the lifted rod;
Ascends to Night's dim, solitary throne,
And clothes it with a splendor not its own-
A ghastly grandeur and a ghostly sheen,
Through which the pale stars tremble as they're seen;

Descends to fire the far horizon's rim,
And paints Mount Etnas in the cloudland grim;
Or, proud to own fair Science' rightful sway,
Low bends along th' electric wire to play,
And, helping out the ever-wondrous plan,
Becomes, in sooth, an errand-boy for man!

This Power it was, which, not content with aught
As yet achieved by human will or thought,
Disdained the slow account of months or days,
In navigation of the ocean ways,
And days would shorten into hours, and these
To minutes, in the face of sounding seas.
If Thought might not be borne upon the foam
Of furrowing keel, with speed that Thought should roam,
It then should walk, like light, the ocean's bed,
And laugh to scorn the winds and waves o'er head!
Beneath the reach of storm or wreck, down where
The skeletons of men and navies are,
Its silent steps should be; while o'er its path
The monsters of the deep, in sport or wrath,
The waters lashed, till like a pot should boil
The sea, and fierce Arion seize the upcast spoil.

America! to thee belongs the praise
Of this great crowning deed of modern days.
'T was Franklin called the wonder from on high;
'T was Morse who bade it on man's errands fly—
'T was he foretold its pathway 'neath the sea:
A daring Field fulfilled the prophecy!
'T was fitting that a great, free land like this,
Should give the lightning's voice to Liberty;
Should wing the heralds of Earth's happiness,
And sing, beneath the ever-sounding sea,
The fair, the bright millennial days to be.

Now may, ere long, the sword be sheathed to rust,
The helmet laid in undistinguished dust;
The thund'rous chariot pause in mid career,
Its crimsoned wheels no more through blood to steer;
The red-hoofed steed from fields of death be led,
Or turned to pasture where the armies bled;
For Nation unto Nation soon shall be
Together brought in knitted unity,
And man be bound to man by that strong chain,
Which, linking land to land, and main to main,
Shall vibrate to the voice of Peace, and be
A throbbing heartstring of Humanity!

FAITH.

FAIR Queen of this May Day ! the tributes I bring
Are not from the regions where Cherubim sing,
Or glory refulgent encircles the throne
Of Him, the Almighty, th' Eternal; the One.
Though there is the home of my ultimate rest,
A Paradise endless, surpassingly blest,
Yet Earth was my birth-place, my mission is here,
And dear is that birth-place, that mission is dear.
'Tis true I was born in the wisdom of God,
And though of the earth not akin to the sod,
'Tis mine to give comfort when sadness doth reign,
And draw from the bosom the sting of its pain;
For hope .to the hopeless I whispering send,
And show the despondent a heavenly friend.
Oh sad was the world ere my spirit began,
To give forth its balm and its fragrance to man,
For wild was the trouble and darksome the grief
Which had in kind Heaven no trust or belief.
'Tis Faith in the heart that giveth to life

The peace of the home-hearth, the joys of the wife,
'Tis Faith that entrances with gladness the lover,
Who trusts in his idol, knows nothing above her,
And sees her grow beautiful, ever and ever.
'Tis Faith in our fellows, their goodness and truth
That makes the chief glory of childhood and youth;
And cursed is the soul with a withering ban
That has lived till it trusteth no longer in Man.
The gifts that I bring thee, so still must I say,
Are not the far gems that bediamond the way
Where star-crowned immortals beatified stray.
They're relics I've gathered along the dim shore
Of life and of time—these are all—nothing more.
This fragment that's rusted, 'Tis all that remains
Of the heroes' and martyrs' rude fetters and chains;
This ring, 'Twas the sign, on a hand that is dust,
Of love that was sacred, and holiest trust;
These pearls that so glisten like crystalline spheres,
They are the congealment of penitent tears.
Oh skeptic, sore-hearted, accept them I pray,
For healing is in them, and blessing for aye.

HUMBOLDT RIVER.[4]

THE River of Death, as it rolls
With a sound like the wailing of souls!
And guarding their dust, may be seen
The ghosts of the dead by the green
Billowy heaps on the shore—
Dim shapes, as they crouch by the graves,
And wail with the rush of the waves

---

[4] For three hundred miles its banks are one continuous burying ground. Emigrants to California died on its shores by thousands.

On seeking the desert before I
Guarding their dust for the morn
Which shall see us, new-born
Arise from the womb of the earth—
That, through rain or through dearth,
Through calm or through storm,
Through seasons and times, no part may be lost,
By the ruthless winds tost,
Of the mortal which shall be immortal of form.

No leaf that may bud
By that dark sullen flood;
No flower that may bloom
With its tomb-like perfume,
In that region infectious of gloom;
No subtleized breath
That may ripple that River of Death,
Or, vapory, float in the desolate air,
But is watched with a vigilant, miserly care,
Lest it steal from the dust of the dead that are there;
For the elements aye are in league,
With a patience unknowing fatigue,
To scatter mortality's mould,
And sweep from the graves what they hold!

I would not, I ween, be the wight
To roam by that river at night,
When the souls are abroad in the glooms;
Enough that the day-time is weird
With the mystical sights that are feared
Mid the silence of moonlighted tombs;
Weird shores with their alkaline white—
That loom in the glare of the light;
Weird bones as they bleach in the sun,
Where the beast from his labors is done;
Weird frost-work of poisonous dews

On shrub and on herb, which effuse
The death they have drank to the core;
Weird columns upborne from the floor
Of the white-crusted deserts which boil
With the whirlwind's hot, blasting turmoil!
As ghost-like he glides on his way.
Each ghastly, worn pilgrim looks gray
With the dust the envenomed winds flail;
And the beast he bestrides is as pale
As the steed of the vision of John,
With him, the Destroyer, thereon.

Dark river, foul river, 'Tis well
That into the jaws of thy Hell—
The open-mouthed desert[5]—should fall
Thy waves that so haunt and appall.
'Tis fit that thou seek the profound
Of all-hiding Night underground;
Like the river which nine times around
The realm of grim Erebus wound,
To roll in that region of dread—
A Stygian stream of the Dead!

TO A YOUNG LADY.

DEEP in thy heart is slumbering Love,
   Oh maiden of the sweet blue eye!
And with him on his crimson couch
   All tenderest of Graces lie.

---

[5]   Sink of the Humboldt

His breathings through thy parted lips
   Are balmy as the breeze that blows
From islands of the Indian seas,
   And with their light and bloom he glows.

I hear him whispering of the dreams
   He dreams! he whispers soft and low,
Like murmurings on some pearly strand,
   Where rippling waters come and go.

He breathed no name, but there is one
   Whom he and all the gods adore;
The bright ideal one, the strong, the brave,
   Who yet shall come from Heaven's own shore.

Oh hearts of roses! lily's lives!
   To wed with him were bliss divine,
Oh happy husbands, happy wives,
   If souls were all like his and thine!

TO A STAR SEEN AT TWILIGHT.

HAIL solitary star!
That shinest from thy far blue height,
And overlookest Earth
And Heaven, companionless in light!
The rays around thy brow
Are an eternal wreath for thee;
Yet thou'rt not proud, like man,
Though thy broad mirror is the sea,
And thy calm home eternity!

Shine on, night-bosomed star!
And through its realms thy soul's eye dart,

TO A STAR SEEN AT TWILIGHT

And count each age of light,
For their eternal wheel thou art.

Thou dost roll into the past days,
Years, and ages too,
And naught thy giant progress stays.

I love to gaze upon
Thy speaking face, thy calm, fair brow,
And feel my spirit dark
And deep, grow bright and pure as thou.
Like thee it stands alone;
Like thee its native home is night,
But there the likeness ends,—
It beams not with thy steady light.
Its upward path is high,
But not so high as thine—thou'rt far
Above the reach of clouds,
Of storms, of wreck, oh lofty star!
I would all men might look
Upon thy pure sublimity,
And in their bosoms drink
Thy lovliness and light like me;
For who in all the world
Could gaze upon thee thus, and feel
Aught in his nature base,
Or mean, or low, around him steal!

Shine on companionless
As now thou seem'st. Thou art the throne
Of thy own spirit, star!
And mighty things must be alone.
Alone the ocean heaves,
Or calms his bosom into sleep;
Alone each mountain stands
Upon its basis broad and deep;
Alone through heaven the comets sweep,

Those burning worlds which God has thrown
Upon the universe in wrath,
As if he hated them—their path
No stars, no suns may follow, none—
'Tis great, 'Tis great to be alone!

REMEMBRANCE OF A SUMMER'S NIGHT.

    THE evening's air breathed softly o'er
A silent spot in midst of sylvan scene,
    Where, bounded by a flow'ry shore,
A cool, fresh lakelet spread its polished sheen;
    Alone, with book of ancient lore
I patient sat and mused on what hath been.

    The shadows of the mossy pine,
That o'er the quiet depths in silence fell,
    Seemed like some spirit's wing divine,
Which, hovering there, shed round a holy spell;
    And, while I read each storied line,
It seemed within my heart of hearts to dwell.

    With noiseless steps the moments came,
And still unheard they went; the softened light
    In mellow rays fell o'er each name
Renowned, a heavenly tribute rich and bright;
    Still o'er the records grand of fame
I looked, nor marked the soft approach of Night.

    She came unheralded by sound,
And stole upon me like a dream; the leaves
    Grew dim, and when I gazed around,
Behold! the mystic curtain that she weaves
    To hide from day her silent bound,
Hung far away to where Old Ocean heaves.

REMEMBRANCE OF A SUMMER'S NIGHT

Where wing'd imagination roams
On high the moon in saint-like beauty rose,
    And in their pure ethereal domes
The kingly stars sat throned in grand repose—
    As calm those worlds as might the homes
Of angels be, where love immortal grows.

Wrapt "in the mantle of the dark,"
Against an aged tree my form I leant,
    And gazed upon each shining mark
That night had placed upon her steep ascent,
    From fitful flash of meteor spark
To worlds beneath whose weight the heavens are bent.

So deep the quiet of the spot,
So broad the mystery of silence spread,
    It seemed that from my earthly lot
I rose to mingle with the mighty dead,
    Whose steadfast thrones time reaches not,
And round whose brows eternal light is shed.

Far borne into the midst of space,
Methought I heard the wheels of ages roll,
    And whisperings of another race
Whose language seemed familiar to my soul;
    And beauteous night from this high place
Far spread her broad, illuminated scroll.

Upon that mighty page unrolled
I read, bright syllabled in blazing spheres,
    What science hath but feebly told
In all the wisdom of her garnered years;
    For science halts, where strong and bold
Imagination soars, and scorns all fears.

Sad seemed the star-typed record there,
Where, through the blinding mists and tearful gloom,
   All dimly burned our world so fair,
Our wondrous world of sorrow, sin and doom!
   In sable stoled—and grim despair
Sat on her brow as raven on a tomb.

   Pale thoughts around her, like a host
Of thronging shadows, veiled her sorrowing head—
   Remembrance of her Eden lost,
The guiltless blood upon her bosom shed,
   Her generations that were dust,
Her millions that were yet to join the dead!

   Mid all the congregated lights
That pendant in the silver concave shone,
   Or crowned with fire the golden heights
That rose like altars to a GOD UNKNOWN,
   Her light was saddest, and the night's
Slow tears that fell seemed wept for her alone.

   Mid all the princely orbs, that bowed
In mute obesiance to their Monarch sun,
   Or, with his primal force endowed,
In paths of circling glory round him run;
   Mid all the constellated crowd
Thick strewn by Him, the wonder-working ONE.

   Upon his world-creating path,
'Twas strange, methought, this beauteous earth alone
   Should thus draw down selectest wrath,
And in her heart of fire for ages groan;
   That here alone should sorrow scathe,
And mouldy Death erect his ghastly throne!

REMEMBRANCE OF A SUMMER'S NIGHT

    But higher yet I seemed to soar
And pierced the visual dome in upward flight,
    As if through angel-opened door
Had passed a soul untombed from vaulted night,
    And stood where ne'er it stood before
In lowly worship of the new-born light.

    'Twas glorious thus in dreams to tread
The supra mortal realms—abodes where none
    Earth-born can enter, save the dead—
Who mate with essences the living shun;
    Those beautiful, pale forms of dread
The gifted see, ere their brief day is done.

    'Twas thus my soul did wander far,
The finite in the infinite, and, wild
    With ecstasy, from star to star,
And from the constellations vast uppiled
    On pillared worlds (that pendant are)
To orbic systems, vaster still, which smiled

    In rays eternal from a height
Of heights immeasurable, did climb! And still
    Did climb the upward maze of light,
As if despite the interdicting will
    That quelled the Babel-builders' might,
'T would reach where sat the enthroned INVISIBLE!

    Thus on that summer's night I dreamed,
Till half the stars went down; and to my tent
    Retired: but every orb that beamed
Upon the lonely watches I had spent,
    Was in my soul ensphered, and gleamed
Above my sleep a pictured firmament!

TO LIZZIE.[6]

A WANDERER from my distant, home,
   From those who blest me with their love,
With boundless plains beneath my feet,
   And foreign skies my head above;

I look around me sternly here,
   And smother feelings strong and deep,
While o'er my brow are gathering dark
   The thoughts that from my spirit leap.

I think of her whose bosom sweet,
   Has pillowed oft my sleeping head,
Whose eye would brighten at my voice,
   Whose ear was quick to know my tread.

I think of her, the fondly loved,
   Whose blood and soul have mixed with mine,
Till life had nothing more to give,
   Yet asked of Heaven no boon divine.

Of her whose fitful fate I held,
   As Heaven doth hold a trembling star,
Whose smiles were mine, whose tears were mine,
   And hopes and joys to "make or mar."

Oh lovely one, that pines for me!
   How well she soothed each maddened thought,
And from the ruins of my soul
   A fair and beauteous fabric wrought!

---

[6] Written on the Plains.

Whose base was strong, unshaken faith—
  The boon to mightier spirits given—
Whose towering dome was human love,
  That rose from earth and lived in Heaven!

Ah, best beloved that weeps for me!
  How oft beneath my spirit's wing
I've borne her through the worlds of thought,
  And showed her there each holy thing;

Have caught the fire of themes sublime,
  And wrapt her in their glorious light,
Till in her loftiness of mind,
  She stood an angel in my sight!

How beautiful the hours with her,
  How full of deep, o'erpowering bliss,
When bosoms that so loved were joined,
  And lips that thirsted for the kiss!

Unmindful then of aught but joy,
  'Twas death to gaze and not to meet;
All! all the same if fortune smiled,
  Or ruin yawned beneath our feet!

Ah beautiful! thrice beautiful!
  And passion bound me in her thrall—
In manhood's might before her shrine
  I knelt me down and yielded all.

Then let it go. If I have sinned,
  'Twas that my heart knew no control,
When she that called me to her arms
  Was first, was all that stirred my soul.

THE FORGIVEN DEAD.

PALE lies she now before me,
   Whom late I scorned with bitter sneers,
What spell is this comes o'er me,
   That all mine anger disappears?

My yesterday was clouded
   With thinking of her cruel wrong—
But, white in death thus shrouded,
   I only know I *loved her long* !

'T was not *herself* that wandered;
   It was the demon of her brain—
I scarce can mourn I squandered
   Such love on one whom love hath slain.

For died she not, pain-haunted
   That truth she had forsook for gold?
Death, thou hast disenchanted
   Her of sin—chaste, beautiful and cold!

But yesterday I wept not,
   As pined she on her costly bed;
Well know I now, she slept not
   There in peace, till slept she—dead!

I do forgive her, wholly;
   Ye angels hear me—I forgive!
She lies so sweet and lowly—
   She could not bear to sin and live.

To strew her tomb with roses,
   Pure-white, as virgins' tombs should be,
I had not thought: but Fate disposes—
   Her soul was virgin unto *me*.

TO A MOCKING BIRD SINGING IN A TREE.

SING on thou little mocker, sing—
  Sarcastic Poet of the bowery clime!
Though full of scoff thy notes are sweet
  As ever filled melodious rhyme!
I love thee for thy gracefulness,
  And for thy jollity—such happiness!
Oh, I could seize it for my booty
  But that the deed would make thy music less.

Say, now, do not the feathery bands
  Feel hatred for thy songs which mock their own!
And as thou passest by, revile
  Thee angrily, with envy in their tone?
Or, are their little breasts too pure
  To know the pangs our human bosoms feel?
Perhaps they love thee for that same,
  And from thy sweetness new heart-gushes steal?

Upon the summit of yon tree
  How gaily thou dost sing! how free from pain.
Oh; would that my sad heart could bound
  With half the Eden rapture of thy strain!
I then would mock at every tear
  That falls where sorrow's shaded fountains flow,
And smile at every sigh that heaves
  In dark regret o'er some bewildering woe.

But mine is not thy breast—nor would
  I place within its little core one sting
That goads my own, for all the bliss
  That heartless robbery of thee Would bring.
Ah no, still keep thy music power
  The ever radiant glory of thy soul,

And let thy voice of melody
    Soar on, as now, abhorrent of control.

May be thou sing'st of heaven sometimes,
    As raptured consciousness vades thy breast;
May be of some far home where love
    O'er bird-land spreads soft cooling shades of rest.
If man, whose voice is far less sweet
    Than thine, looks high for his eternal home,
Oh, say, do not thy dreamings too
    For some green spot and habitation roam?

If living thought can never die,
    Why should thine own expire? If there is love
Within thy heart, it must live on,
    Nor less than man's have dwelling-place above;
Thy notes shall then be brighter far
    Than now they be! And I may listen, too,
With finer ear, and clearer soul,
    Beneath a shade more soft, a sky more blue.

MARY, QUEEN OF SCOTS.

ALAS, that aught of sin or shame
Should cling around thy gentle name,
Or sorrow with thy mem'ry twine,
Mid roses fair, its poisoned vine!
Beloved of heaven, that made thee fair—
Earth's favorite child I who gave to thee
Her choicest gifts of beauty rare,
How couldst thou aught but happy be?
Yet sadness round thy earlier years
Its ever varying shadows threw.

And midst a world of torturing fears,
Thy trembling womanhood upgrew.
Though rainbows many arched thy path,
They shone amid thy numerous tears,
And stood beneath a sky of wrath.
Though wronged so deeply that mankind
Indignant reads the tale of blood,
Yet thou through mad ambition blind,
Or borne by love's resistless flood,
Too oft did'st do and sanction wrong.
Alas, that crime thy bosom knew!
The Poet mourns it in his song,
And Hist'ry weeps to write it true.

A CHEROKEE LOVE SONG.

OH COME with me by moonlight, love,
    And let us seek the river's shore;
My light canoe awaits thee, love,
    The sweetest burden e'er it bore!

The soft, low winds are whispering there
    Of human beauty, human love,
And with approving faces, too,
    The stars are shining from above.

Come place thy small white hand in mine,
    My boat is 'neath those willow trees,
And with my practised arm, the oar
    Will ask no favor from the breeze.

Now, now we're on the waters, love,
    Alone upon the murmuring tide—
Alone! but why should we regret,
    If there were none on earth beside?

What matters it, if all were gone?
   Thy bird-like voice could yet beguile,
And earth were heaven's substitute,
   If thou were left to make it smile!

Oh, mark how soft the dipping oar,
   That silent cleaves the yielding blue—
Oh list, the low, sweet melody
   Of waves that beat our vessel too!

Oh, look to heaven, how pure it seems,
   No cloud to dim, no blot, no stain,
And say—if we refuse to love,
   Ought we to hope or smile again?

That island green, with roses gemmed,
   Let 's seek it, love—how sweet a spot?
Then let the hours of night speed on,
   We live to love—it matters not!

DEDICATION FOR AN ALBUM.

THESE leaves to friendship consecrate
   And pure affection's holy trust,
You ask me now to dedicate
   In form that's due—and so I must.

I would some worthier hand than mine
   The task essayed; for I profane,
With words that shame the sacred Nine,
   The page that else had known no stain.

Yet e'en the rudest terms of speech
   Are hallowed by the truth they breathe;

And so these lines that nothing teach,
   May dare this shrine of love enwreath.

Blest be each spotless page herein,
   Whereon the hand of love shall write,
And worthy of the place they win
   The names that here shall meet the sight.

So that, fair owner of this book,
   When you these leaves shall wander through
In after years, and pause to look
   On name and date no longer new,

A buried past will seem to be
   Within the pages that you turn;
And sweet but mournful memory
   Will linger o'er each hallowed urn.

THE RAINY SEASON IN CALIFORNIA.

THE rains have come, the winds are shrill,
   Dark clouds are trailing near the ground;
The mists have clothed each naked hill,
   And all is sad and drear around.

The swollen torrents rapid rush,
   Far down the mountain gorges deep;
Now, falling o'er the jagged rocks,
   They thunder through the hollows steep.

Now, in a basin boiling round,
   They dance in maddest music high,
Or, with a sudden leap or bound,
   Dash on like bolts of destiny.

From mountain's side to mountain's side,
  The chasms vast in vapors lost,
Seem like a sea of darkness wide,
  Which fancy dreams can ne'er be crost.

Far off the loftier mountains stand,
  Calm, saint-like in their robes of white,
Like heaven-descended spirits grand
  Who fill the darkness with their light.

Black clouds are rolling round their feet,
  And ever strive to higher climb,
But still their mists dissolve in rain,
  And reach not to that height sublime.

Gone are the birds with sunny days,
  But flowers shall cheer us in their room,
And shrubs that pined in summer rays
  Shall top their leafy boughs with bloom.

The grass grows green upon the hills,
  (Now wrapt in thickly fallen clouds),
Which tall and beautiful shall rise
  When they have cast their wintry shrouds.

Then wandering through their thousand vales,
  Each flowery bordered path shall lead
To gardens wild, where nature's hand
  Hath nurtured all with kindly heed.

Her own voluptuous couch is spread
  Beneath the curtains of the sky,
And on her soft and flowery bed
  The night looks down with loving eye.

THE RAINY SEASON IN CALIFORNIA

But Fancy paints the scene too fast,
    For thus she always loves to leave
The bitter present or the past,
    And rainbows from the future weave.

Lo I night upon my musings here,
    With rapid, stealthy foot hath crept
Unheard amid the sullen sounds
    Which o'er my head have lately swept.

The pouring rain upon the roof,
    The winds in wild careering bands,
Seem bent to see if tempest proof
    The building on its basis stands.

The fiend of this dark night and storm
    Stands howling at my very door—
I dread to see her haggard form
    Break in and pass the threshold o'er.

But hold your own my trusty door!
    Yield not an inch to's utmost might,
Nor let the hellish wild uproar
    That reigns without come in to-night.

It stands—my lonely candle burns,
    The single light for miles around;
Reminding me of some, last hope
    That still will light life's gloom profound.

Howl on ye elemental sprites,
    And mutter forth your curses deep,
The anarchy that others frights,
    Shall rock me soundly into sleep.

For, oh, I love to slumber 'neath
   The tempest's wrathful melody,
And dream all night that on its wings
   My soul enchanted soareth free.

THE HARP OF BROKEN STRINGS.

A STRANGER in a stranger land,
   Too calm to weep, too sad to smile,
I take my harp of broken strings,
   A weary moment to beguile;
And tho no hope its promise brings,
   And present joy is not for me,
Still o'er that harp I love to bend,
   And feel its broken melody
With all my shattered feelings blend.

I love to hear its funeral voice
   Proclaim how sad my lot, how lone;
And when, my spirit wilder grows,
   To list its deeper, darker tone.
And when my soul more madly glows
   Above the wrecks that round it lie,
It fills me with a strange delight,
   Past mortal bearing, proud and high,
To feel its music swell to might.

When beats my heart in doubt and awe,
   And Reason pales upon her throne,
Ah, then, when no kind voice can cheer
   The lot too desolate, too lone,
Its tones come sweet upon my ear,
   As twilight o'er some landscape fair
     As light upon the wings of night

THE HARP OF BROKEN STRINGS

(The meteor flashes in the air,
   The rising stars) its tones are bright.

And now by Sacramento's stream,
   What mem'ries sweet its music brings—
The vows of love, its smiles and tears,
   Hang o'er this harp of broken strings.
It speaks, and midst her blushing fears
   The beauteous one before me stands!
Pure spirit in her downcast eyes,
   And like twin doves her folded hands!

It breathes again—and at my side
   She kneels, with grace divinely rare—
Then showering kisses on my lips,
   She hides our busses with her hair;
Then trembling with delight, she flings
   Her beauteous self into my arms,
As if o'erpowered, she sought for wings
   To hide her from her conscious charms.

It breathes once more, and bowed in grief,
   The bloom has left her cheek forever,
While, like my broken harp-strings now,
   Behold her form with feeling quiver!
She turns her face o'errun with tears,
   To him that silent bends above her,
And, by the sweets of other years,
   Entreats him still, oh, still to love her!

He loves her still—but darkness falls
   Upon his ruined fortunes now,
And 'T is his exile doom to flee.
   The dews, like death, are on his brow,
And cold the pang about his heart
   Oh, cease—to die is agony:
'T is more than death when loved ones part!

Well may this harp of broken strings
   Seem sweet to me by this lonely shore.
When like a spirit it breaks forth,
   And speaks of beauty evermore!
When like a spirit it evokes
   The buried joys of early youth,
And clothes the shrines of early love,
   With all the radiant light of truth!

OCTOBER HILLS.

I LOOK upon the purple hills
   That rise in steps to yonder peaks,
And all my soul their silence thrills
   And to my heart their beauty speaks.

What now to me the jars of life,
   Its petty cares, its harder throes?
The hills are free from toil and strife,
   And clasp me in their deep repose.

They soothe the pain within my breast
   No power but theirs could ever reach,
They emblem that eternal rest
   We cannot compass in our speech.

From far I feel their secret charm—
   From far they shed their healing balm,
And lost to sense of grief or harm
   I plunge within their pulseless calm.

How full of peace and strength they stand,
   Self-poised and conscious of their weight

We rise with them, that silent band,
   Above the wrecks of Time or Fate;

For, mounting from their depths unseen,
   Their spirit pierces upward, far,
A soaring pyramid serene,
   And lifts us where the angels are.

I would not lose this scene of rest,
   Nor shall its dreamy joy depart;
Upon my soul it is imprest,
   And pictured in my inmost heart.

THE MAID OF THE MOUNTAINS.

As PURE as the snowflake that melts on her lips,
   As the wind like a lover she meets at the door,
And as sweet as the roses, as o'er them she trips,
   That blush at revealments ne'er charmed them before,

Is the Maid of the Mountain, their pride and their boast
   Her face like the morning, her hair like the night,
Her eye like the eve-star that mellows our coast,
   As tender in beauty, as strong in its light.

We met by the river, that maiden and I,
   Which flows by yon snow-peaks engirdled with pines—
It was a rare meeting for no one was nigh,
   And love had quite lost us mid blossom and vines.

I had but to murmer what well she believed—
   Her answer came leaping to lips and to eyes,
And heart spoke to heart, as her white bosom heaved
   With rapture that knoweth no language but sighs.

Around us and o'er us the humming bird flew,
  As envious he were of her honey-dew kiss:
I whispered her so, and her lips the more grew
  To mine own, rewarding ray praises with bliss.

Oh Eden-like moments, how soon were they fled!
  For sunlight no longer was lighting the stream;
But silver-winged twilight descended instead,
  With mistiness veiled like an angel in dream.

She rose to depart, (my angel) where I,
  Accurs't by the Fates, was forbidden to go;
Sweet cot on the hillside, blessed river near by,
  That mirrors no beauty like her's in its flow!

She rose to depart, and my heart was awake
  To glory new-born in her steps as she went.
Her stately obeisance the lily did make,
  And sweetest of blue-bells in reverence bent.

Ah, well might they worship a vision so bright,
  No being of earth could they deem her to be,
But they have forgotten their passing delight,
  While the pang of the parting still lingers with me.

ON YUBA CITY.

The Yuba City silent stands
  Where Providence has placed her,
The glory 's passed to other hands,
  That should by right have graced her.

ON YUBA CITY

She stands with aspect sad but high,
   And gazes on the river,
That like a stranger passes by,
   And nothing has to give her.

Alas, that beauty thus should fade,
   Or live so unregarded!
And all the efforts art has made
   Or her, pass unrewarded!

Are not her groves most fair to see,
   Her paths full greenly skirted?
What has she said, or done, to be
   Thus doomed, and thus deserted?

Though melancholy her decline,
   By mem'ries sweet 'T is haunted,
And luring tones and forms divine
   Still make her scenes enchanted.

There, peace domestic reigns supreme,
   In quiet, holy beauty,
And like the smiles of angels, seem
   Parental, filial duty.

Her aged ones are good and mild,
   Her children fair and witty.
But Caroline's the *fairest child*
   That charms the lonely city!

I've seen her at the morning prime—
   The sky looked sweeter, bluer!
I've seen her at the evening time—
   The stars seemed bending to her!

Oh, Yuba City ! 'Tis a sin
  Thou 'rt lonely and forsaken,
When uglier cities favor win,
  And prosperous paths have taken.

Who seeks for beauty, they shall meet
  The picture where they find thee—
The Feather River at thy feet,
  The lofty Buttes behind thee.

And they will bless the quiet scene
  That holds thee like a jewel,
And weep that thou 'st abandoned been
  To fortunes cold and cruel.

But, Yuba City, time will cast
  The changes in thy favor,
The future shall redeem the past—
  Thou 'lt stand whilst others waver!

OF HER I LOVE.

I READ but a moment her beautiful eyes,
  I glanced at the charm of her snowy-white hand
I caught but the glimpse of her cheek's blushing dyes
  More sweet than the fruits of a tropical land;

I marked but an instant her coral-hued lips,
  And the row of sweet pearls that glimmered between—
Those lips, like the roses the humming bird sips
  On his bright wing of rainbows, when summer is green.

I timidly gazed on a bosom more white
  Than the breast of the swan, more soft than its down—
To rest on whose pillows were greater delight
  Than all else of rapture that heaven may own.

I gazed but a second on these, and on all
  That make up the sum of her angel-like form,
And ere I could think I was bound in her thrall,
  And peace fled my breast, as the birds flee a storm!

I am bound in love's pain, and may never be free,
  Till the bond is dissolved in her own melting kiss:
Till her loveliness, like the embrace of a sea,
  Enclasps me, and hides me in the depths of its bliss.

TO THE BEAUTIFUL.

Ox, blame me not that I am bold,
  Nor scorn my too adventurous rhymes,
For how can he be tame or cold
  Whose heart bath bloomed in southern climes?

Or who bath lived among the flowers,
  Or by those clear perennial streams,
Whose music charms the gliding hours,
  Nor gave his soul to passion's dreams?

Why should his heart not love to live
  Within the light of beauty's eyes,
And all its world of feeling give,
  To win from her, her trembling sighs?

Alas, the world may say 'T is wrong,
  But who can rule the wayward heart?

For we are weak, and nature strong,
   And love is our immortal part!

We may not see the rosy mouth,
   The laughing eye, the graceful limb,
And bosom, like the sunny south,
   With love o'erflowing from the brim.

We may not see such loveliness,
   Without the wish at least to gaze;
And cold were she, denying this
   To him whose every look is praise.

Forgive me, if my heart has erred,
   In deeming thou would'st not despise,
And I will cancel every word,
   To meet forgiveness from thine eyes.

A NIGHT SCENE.

UNBROKEN silence! save the melody
   That steals on silence unawares, and makes
   It seem scarce more than silence still; that takes
Possession of the senses bodily,
   And claims the slumbering spirit ere it wakes.

Save this low melody of waves, no sound
   Is heard among the circling hills. I sit
   And muse alone—the time and place are fit—
And summon spirits from the blue profound,
   That answer me and through my vision flit.

A NIGHT SCENE

What beauteous being stands upon yon hill,
   With hair night-hued, and brow and bosom white?
   Around her floats the evening's loving light—
Her feet are lost amid the shadows soft and still,
   But 'gainst the sky her form is pictured to my sight.

How still! how motionless! yet full of life,
   As is of music-tones the sleeping string,
   As is of grace the blue-bird's resting wing!
She pauses there—each limb with beauty rife—
   As if through a boundless space her foot might spring.

But hark what tones are filling all the air,
   That drinks them, with the star-light blended now,
   And wavelet-murmurings from below?
Her voice! her harp! swept by the white hand rare
   That moon-like guides the music's tide-like flow.

Strange one ! no voice I've heard like thine,
   No startling beauty like thine own have seen,
   The rounded world and vaulted heaven between.
To gaze on thee 'Tis madness all divine,
   But o'er the gulf my spirit loves to lean.

Thou art what I may ne' er embrace on earth,
   Thou sweetly moulded one, thou heavenly-eyed!
   But if when we do lay these forms aside,
For us new forms among the stars have birth
   In some sweet world we'll meet, my spirit bride!

Fair worlds, like ripples o'er the watery deep
   When breezes softly o'er the surface play,
   In circles one by one ye stretch away,
Till, lost to human vision's wildest sweep
   Our souls are left to darkness and dismay.

ODE TO THE NATIONAL FLAG.

Oh star-gemmed banner of the free,
   Thou streamest still on high,
A living beacon to the world,
   The glory of our sky.

To thee the gazing millions turn,
   With patriot hopes and fears,
Brave men with burning glance uplift,
   Fair women with their tears.

As blazing in the van of war,
   As flashing in its cloud,
Amid the rolling thunders' peals,
   We call to thee aloud.

Oh! banner that our fathers loved,
   That shadows yet their graves
Still with thy strong winged eagle speed
   Where the tempests brave.

Oh never may thy stars go down,
   Or in the battle pale;
Or hands grow weak that bear thee up.
   Or hearts beneath thee quail.

As on the flaming war-tide borne
   And in its hot breath tost.
Now seen amidst the rifled gloom,
   Now in the darkness lost.

Oh how we watch where yet thou art,
   As on the battle wears,
And rising, sinking, follow thee
   With thousand, thousand prayers.

ODE TO THE NATIONAL FLAG

Those prayers, O God shall not be vain—
   Descended from the sky,
With bosom bared, and sword of fire
   Upleaping from her thigh,

A new Minerva treads the plain;
   She snatches from the gloom
Her country's flag and bears it
   As with the Step of doom.

Ah well she knows, fair Liberty,
   How sacred is the name
Of that, her conquering arm defends,
   How glorious is its fame.

And not unused unto the strife
   Where deeds for Right are done,
The earthquake which her cradle rocked
   Saw birth of Washington.

In that great name and in her own,
   She bares her arm for blood,
And bending to the fates on high,
   She strikes for man and God.

Thus, holy flag into her hand
   Thy future's all we give,
Assured thou canst not stoop to dust,
   While she herself shall live!

To C——.

Thou bring'st me back the golden days
   Of youth's bright dreams and fancies,
When life was full of pleasant ways,
   And all its scenes seemed romances.

Thou mind'st me of the angel-forms
   That thronged the heaven above me,
As lay I midst the summer's charms,
   And deemed that one. might love me.

Thou hast her fine and airy shape,
   Her brow of tranquil sweetness,
Her large blue orbs, whence did escape
   Such changing beams of fleetness.

Thou hast her ripe and rosy mouth,
   So doubly sweet in smiling,
Where kisses sunny as the South,
   Lay slumbering but beguiling.

Thou hast her step of lightsome grace,
   Eve-like ere Eve knew sinning;
The virgin, beauty of a face
   That knows not it is winning.

Oh, for my youth time what a prize!
   Too late rare girl I find thee—
My dream not I must realize—
   No bond of mine can bind thee.

ROSA DUNN.

I'll tell thee of a maiden fair,
   A bird of beauty, child of fun,
A living joy is in her air,
   And her sweet name is Rosa Dunn.

Her winning mouth and laughing eye
   Have lovers wounded, many a one,
And hundreds now are fain to die
   For her dear sake, bright Rosa Dunn.

Where'er she moves to her rare form
   Are all pure sweets and beauties won,
And, blent with every glowing charm,
   All nature breathes in Rosa Dunn.

She walks at morning mid the flowers,
   And drinks their freshness like the sun,
And all the blooms of Eden bowers
   Are in the cheeks of Rosa Dunn.

The rose she kisses leaves its red
   Upon those lips no bee would shun;
And all the roses that are dead
   Have died to live in Rosa Dunn.

If roams she 'neath the evening light
   The stars her beauty smile upon;
The love and tenderness of night
   Are in the eyes of Rosa Dunn.

A twin Aurora of the Dawn,
   Until she rise no Day 's begun,
And Night and Day to me are gone,
   When sleep enfoldeth Rosa Dunn.

FALSE, BUT BEAUTIFUL.

DARK as a demon's dream is one I love—
In soul-but oh, how beautiful in form!
She glows like Venus throned in joy above,
Or on the crimson couch of Evening warm
Reposing her sweet limbs, her heaving breast
Unveiled to him who lights the golden west
Ah, me, to be by that soft hand carest,
To feel the twining of that snowy arm,
To drink that sigh with richest love opprest,
To bathe within that sunny sea of smiles,
To wander in that wilderness of wiles
And blissful blandishments—it is to thrill
With subtle poison, and to feel the will
Grow weak in that which all the veins doth fill.
Fair sorceress! I know she spreads a net
The strong, the just, the brave to snare ; and yet
My soul cannot, for its own sake, forget
The fascinating glance which flings its chain
Around my quivering heart and throbbing brain,
And binds me to my painful destiny,
As bird, that soars no more on high,
Hangs trembling on the serpent's doomful eye.

TO L—— ON RECEIVING HER PORTRAIT.

LONG years have passed, and I have seen thee not,
   Save in my waking and my nightly dreams,
When rose our quiet well-remembered cot
   In that far land of pleasant woods and streams.

TO L—— ON RECEIVING HER PORTRAIT

Around my brow the storms of thought have swept,
    And o'er my brain their quivering lightnings played,
Yet mem'ry bath survived the shock and kept
    Unharmed the impress which thy love has made.

Disease hath fed upon my frame, and I
    Have deemed it would be sweet to sleep beneath
The sod! I thought of thee, and would not die,
    But struggled wish my pain and conquer'd death.

Within the shadows of the mountains tall,
    Which seemed the wings of grand and gloomy thought,
I've laid me down and dreamed— forgetting all
    Save thee and thy sweet holy love unbought.

Deep in the forests lone and dark I've sat,
    'Till sense and soul were charmed; and I did take
The voice of streams for thine, and dreaming that
    Thyself was there, I wept for joy's own sake.

Oft gazing on the Heavens, I've seen thy form
    Of loveliness far floating midst the blue,
Or lying on the couch of Evening warm,
    Whose blush was like thine own cheeks' rosy hue.

And now that thy fair features meet my eyes,
    Presented lifelike by the skill of art,
I feel a thousand raptures bird-like rise,
    And form sweet music-circles round my heart.

I look again: alas, those eyes are sad
    As lonely stars that in the ocean sit!
Reproach me not, sweet orbs! for life has had
    Few charms for me since last those eyes I met.

I turn away: I cannot bear those eyes
   Of melancholy meaning, calm and deep;
They speak to me of rudely rended ties—
   And life's stern task allows no time to weep.

THE STOLEN WHITE GIRL.

THE prairies are broad, and the woodlands are wide
And proud on his steed the wild half-breed may ride,
With the belt round his waist and the knife at his side.
And no white man may claim his beautiful bride.

Though he stole her away from the land of the whites,
Pursuit is in vain, for her bosom delights
In the love that she bears the dark-eyed, the proud,
Whose glance is like starlight beneath a night-cloud.

Far down in the depths of the forest they'll stray,
Where the shadows like night are lingering all day;
Where the flowers are springing up wild at their feet,
And the voices of birds in the branches are sweet.

Together they'll roam by the streamlets that run,
O'ershadowed at times then meeting the sun—
The streamlets that soften their varying tune,
As up the blue heavens calm wanders the moon!

The contrast between them is pleasing and rare;
Her sweet eye of blue, and her soft silken hair,
Her beautiful waist, and her bosom of white
That heaves to the touch with a sense of delight;

His form more majestic and darker his brow,
Where the sun has imparted its liveliest glow—

An eye that grows brighter with passion's true fire,
As he looks on his loved one with earnest desire.

Oh, never let Sorrow's cloud darken their fate,
The girl of the "pale face," her Indian mate!
But deep in the forest of shadows and flowers,
Let Happiness smile, as she wings their sweet hours.

A JUNE MORNING.

THE MORN is coming o'er the hills
   In vestments rich and rare,
Like girlhood dressed in flowing robes,
   With waves of golden hair.

A blessing's in her hand for man,
   A gift of peace and light;
For while she walks the fields of Heaven
   She plucks their treasures bright.

The birds, those poets of the sky
   Whose voices ne'er grow old,
With gladness sing, and plume their wings
   Of satin and of gold.

The partridge through the thicket runs,
   Clear whistling to his mate—
What knoweth he of grief or pain?
   He never heard of fate!

The deer upon the hills have seen
   The coming of fair morn,
And haste to crop the grass all wet
   With dew-drops from her horn;

The proud old buck with antlered head,
   The nimble-footed doe,
The fawn with eye of innocence
   And skin like calico!

And over all the eagle soars
   In regal majesty,
His gray wing reddening in yon cloud
   That decks the eastern sky;

On mightier wing than aught that flies,
   With keen, far-reaching eye,
He soars like genius in the blaze
   Of Immortality!

And man, whose fancy mounts on high
   E'en where the angels sing,
Immortal man looks up from earth,
   And envies him his wing.

Well may each living thing rejoice,
   For never yet was born,
Beneath the eternal eye of God,
   A fresher, lovelier morn.

THE SABBATH BELLS.

THE Sabbath bells are ringing
   With clear and cheerful notes,
And from the steeple springing,
   Far off the music floats.

THE SABBATH BELLS

To yonder mountains reaches,
   The ever rising strain,
And Echo's dying speeches
   Repeat it o'er again.

The summer woodlands filling,
   The solemn cadence rolls,
And through the leaves is thrilling
   Like soft, pulsating souls.

The air with rippling motion,
   Aeolian answers gives,
And like a trembling ocean,
   Its outspread bosom heaves.

The far horizon sweeping,
   Each tone majestic swells,
And all the world is leaping
   Beneath the sounding bells.

'Tis solemn, yet 'Tis cheerful,
   A clear and pleasant voice,
That bids the sad and tearful
   Be hopeful and rejoice.

Let sabbath morns unclouded
   Still hear these tones of peace,
For earth with woe is shrouded
   When sabbath bells, shall cease.

POEM.[7]

The waves that murmur at our feet,
   Through many an age had rolled
Ere fortune found her favorite seat
   Within this land of gold.

The Digger, searching for his roots,
   Here roamed the region wide—
Or, wearied with the day's pursuits,
   Slept by this restless tide.

The dream of greatness never rose
   Upon his simple brain;
The wealth on which a nation grows,
   And builds its power to reign,

All darkly lay beneath his tread,
   Where many a stream did wind,
Deep slumbering in its yellow bed,
   The charm that rules mankind.

Had he and his dark brethren known
   Of gold the countless worth,
They now beyond that power had grown
   Which sweeps them from the earth.

But happier he perchance, by far,
   Still digging for his roots,
Than thousand paler wanderers are
   Whose toil hath had no fruits.

---

[7]   Delivered at Commencement of Oakland College, California, June 6th 1861.

Still following luck's unsteady star,
   Where'er its light hath gleamed,
To many a gulch and burning bar,
   Which proved not what it seemed.

How wearied they have sat them down,
   To watch the passers by—
The throng that still 'gainst Fortune's frown,
   Their varied "prospects" try.

Behold the active and the young,
   Whose strength not yet doth fail,
And hear them, with a cheerful tongue,
   Encourage those that quail.

With mournful, melancholy look,
   The broken-hearted come,
Whose souls we read as in a book,
   Though shut their lips and dumb!

And mark yon aged, trembling one,
   How weak his step and slow!
Ah, hear him as he totters on,
   Sigh painfully and low!

Far from the peaceful home he left,
   In fever-rage for gold—
Of friends, almost of hope bereft,
   He now is trebly old.

And Fortune often favors not,
   Who most her favors need;
Thus he may wander on forgot,
   While strong ones gain the meed

How many hearts like his have pined,
   As prisoned bird of air,
For sunny homes they left behind,
   And friends who loved them there,

And many a merry heart shall pine,
   Through long and lonesome years,
And watch the light of life decline
   Amidst uncounted tears.

Far off among the mountains stern,
   Shall thousands meet with blight,
And many a raven lock shall turn
   To hairs of frosty white;

And many a lonely grave shall hide
   The mouldering form of him
For whom sad eyes are never dried,
   With age and sorrow dim.

Yet, though the wayside all be strewn
   With sorrows and with graves,
The glory of the race is shown
   By what it does and braves.

What though the desert's mouldering heaps
   Affright the startled eye—
What though in wilds the venturer sleeps,
   His bones uncovered lie,

'Tis not the living that have won
   Alone the victory:
But each dead soldier, too, has done
   His part as loftily.

'Tis they—the living and the dead—
   Who have redeemed our land;
Have cities reared, the arts have spread,
   And placed us where we stand.

As led Adventure bold before,
   The Arts and Learning came;
And now, behold I upon this shore
   They have a place and name.

Where roamed erewhile the rugged bear
   Amid these oaks of green,
And wandering from his mountain lair
   The cougar's steps were seen,

Lo! Peace hath built her quiet nest;
   And "mild-eyed Science" roves,
As was her wont when Greece was blest,
   In Academic groves.

Oh! tranquil be these shades for aye,
   These groves forever green;
And youth and age still bless their day
   That here their steps have been.

May Learning here still have her seat,
   Her empire of the mind
The home of Genius, Wit's Retreat,
   Whate'er is pure refined.

And thus the proudest boast shall be
   Of young Ambition crowned—
"The woods of Oakland sheltered me,
   Their leaves my brow have bound."

ERINNA.[8]

IMAGINATION! rouse thee from repose,
And to our eyes Erinna lost disclose;
Since from the living voice of Time is gone
Her genius-gifted and melodious tone,
And from his starlit page the words are fled
She from her early lyre in wonder shed!
Arouse thee I fling around her fancied form
A glorious hue—- beauty rich and warm.
'Tis done: alone by Lesbos' wave-washed strand
I see her in the pride of beauty stand,
Far gazing where the Aegena waters smile
Around her native home and classic isle.
Soft blow the breezes on her snowy brow,
And stir the folds around her limbs that flow;
Her golden hair's luxuriance on her neck
Falls unregarded down—it needs no check,
For who would comb the plumage of the bird,
Or smooth the dimpling waves by Zephyrs stirred?
Her small white hands are linked beneath her zone,
And 'Tween her sweetly rounded arms are shown
Twin spheres of love and Pleasure's burning throne!
A glow is on her cheeks and fresh her lips
As evening cloud the sun's vermilion tips;
Her clear, bright eye wild wanders o'er the main,
That rolling its blue waves along, a strain
Eternal utters and sublime, to charm
The fair, green isles that o'er its bosom swarm.

---

[8] Erinna, a native of Lesbos and friend of Sappho, died at the early age of nineteen. She is described as a girl of extraordinary beauty and genius, but her works, all except two or three epigrams, have unfortunately perished. (Poets and Poetry of the Ancients. By Wm. Peter, A..M.)

ERINNA

Ah, beautiful indeed! What magic gives
The grace that in her every movement lives?
What power unseen is breathing o'er her face,
Where every lineament divine we trace?
It is the magic Sorcerer never stole
From science dread—the magic of the soul I
It is the power of Genius, Heaven conferred,
Which, though it be unseen and all unheard,
Imparts its own true beauty to the face,
And lends unto the form its bloom and grace.

Erinna, mid the objects Time has cast
His hand upon, thou standest within the past
In lonely and peculiar loveliness.
The child of song, with nature's own impress
Upon thee, yet thy harp is hushed, and no
Sweet strains of thine through distant times shall flow
Thy voice hath perished sweetly though it sung,
And perished those who on its accents hung.

Thou wert a bird that breathed its soul away
In song, and died— but Echo lost the lay;
Thou wert a star which shone a single night,
But, setting once, returned no more its light.
Thou art a glorious image of the mind
Seen through the depths of ages Far behind,
Round which our Fancy flings her brightest beams,
While ancient Story faintly aids her dreams.

The friend of Sappho! linked together be
Those names, and never wrecked on Time's wide sea;
And when we read the passion—wildering strain
Of Sappho's muse, that charms the listening brain,
We'll feel Erinna's voice our hearts inspire,
And deem her lovely hand is on the lyre!

LINES ON A HUMMING BIRD SEEN AT A LADY'S WINDOW

YON dew-drunk bacchanal
Hath emptied all the roses of their sweets,
And drained the fluent souls
Of all the lilies from their crystal bowls;
And now, on rapid wing he fleets
To where by yonder crystal pane
A lady, young and fair,
Looks out upon the sifting sunlit rain.

That ripe, red mouth he takes
For rarer flower than ever yet was quaffed,
And longeth much to sip,
The honey of that warm and dewy lip,
And drain its sweetness at a draught.
Ah, vain, delusive hope! 'Tis hard,
But, rainbow wing-ed bird,
Thou 'rt not alone from those sweet lips debarred.

Now, charm-ed with her eyes,
And dazzled by their more than sunny light,
He winnoweth with his wings
The fineness of the golden mist, and swings,
A breathing glory in her sight!
Too happy bird, he's won a smile
From that proud beauty there
Which from his throne an angel might beguile.

How dizzy with delight
He spins his radiant circles in the air!
Now, on their spiral breath
Upborn, he 'scapes th' enchantress underneath
And will not die of joy or despair—

The joy of her bright eyes, and wild,
Despairing e'er to win.
The nectar of those lips which on him smiled.

CALIFORNIA.

BRIGHT land of summery days and golden peace,
Of vine anti flower and ever rich increase;
Of veined hills and mountains treasure-stoned,
Where miser-gnomes in secret watch their hoard,
And startle at the burglar pick and spade,
That do their careful-hidden wealth invade,
I would some better worthier hand than mine
Could yield thee now the tributes that are thine,
And paint thee, as a poet should, divine!
But, poor indeed would be the tongue, and weak,
Which could not something of thy glories speak.
And while for thee no gems of thought I bring
From starry paths of lonely wandering.
Where Genius wont to stray, yet may my muse
Have found such tribute as thou'lt not refuse—
Some humbler flowers of modest mien and hue
By silver streams in truth's fair fields that grew.

Than this sun lights up no lovelier land,
So wondrous rich and beautiful and grand!
From where Old Ocean 'gainst the rock-bound shore
His billows roll with never-ceasing roar
To where the far-off ghostly snow-realm shines,
Or solemn music of the mountain pines
Sounds through those dim and haunted solitudes,
As if the thunder whispered to the woods;
Or where the golden-sanded streams do stray
And freshen Nature in their gladdening way;

Where'er our footsteps tend our visions roam,
We find but beauty's Eden, grandeur's home!

Yet not alone to Nature's bounteous hand
Are due the glories of this magic land;
For man hath taught its fertile soil to yield
The yellow largess of the waving field,
And give to generous toil as rich guerdon
Of thousand fruits as toil hath ever won.
In deed and truth not idle hath he been—
His busy work is all around us seen.
From north to south, and from the east to west,
His forming, changing hand hath not seen rest.
The Arts and Labor spake, and lo! there rose
(As dream-like as the cloud-born city shows,
At morning in the east) this grandest Queen
Of all the cities of the West. With mien
Majestic as of right her look should be,
She sits like Tyre of old beside the sea;
And, while the messengers of commerce wait,
She opens wide and free her Golden Gate.
From far to her the nations laden come
With silks and wares and precious stones and gum,
And of the spoils she every land beguiles
And ocean yields them from his thousand isles.

Nor less the Genius of the Arts, with aid
Of Labor's rugged toil, hath been displayed
Where, winding through the arid plains and drear
That freshen with the liquid presence near,
Or circling round the pine-clad mountain's side,
With crystal music in its rippling tide,
Or rolling, joyous in its volumed flow,
O'er yawning gulf and deep abyss below,
The sinuous flume far bears its precious stream,
And thousand hearts are gladdened in its gleam!

Nor less where, swift upon his path of fire,
The modern Mercury treads th' electric wire—
The living chord that vibrates through the hills,
Groans in the storms or in the breezes thrills;
Threads plain and wilderness, and pierces far
To homes that nestle where the glaciers are.
Nor less again have Art and Labor wrought
To realize the bold, inventive thought
That finds achievement in the tunneled hills.
The sunken shaft, the thunder of the mills;
The rivers leaping from their ancient bed
And plunging headlong in the course they're led;
The mountains crumbling to the level plain,
And forests prostrate 'neath the ax's reign.

And shall we view these miracles and more
Which mind and muscle never wrought before,
Without remembrance in these latter years,
Of those brave men, those hardy Pioneers,
Who led the way for Science, Art, and Law,
'Mid dangers their successors never saw,
And countless hardships that they never knew?
The famed and unfamed heroes tried and true,
Who crowded into months or days the deeds
Of years, and of young empire sowed the seeds?
Amid the mass there here and there appears
Some reverend head, majestic as a seer's—
Arising from the rest like snow-crowned peak,
Around whose brow' the whitening tempests break!
These are the Pioneers of Pioneers,
Those elder heroes in the fight, who, years
And years agone, did drive the wild beast back
To plant their homes where late he left the track.
They're sinking, one by one, like pines that long
Have braved, erect, the howling winters strong,
To fall at last midst stillest peace profound,

And wake the woods with wonder at the sound.
Shall these old heroes be forgot? Not so,
For, while they yet survive Time's downward flow,
I see a rescuing hand stretched forth to save
The good, the true, from dark Oblivion's grave.
'Tis woman's hand that thus would snatch from night
Those honored names far worthier of the light,
And them transmit to shine on History's scroll
When that gray sage his records shall unroll.
And yet some whom the weeping muse laments,
Have their unwrit but lasting monuments.
Such is that Peak which bears brave Lassen's name—
A fit memorial of the grandest fame;
For it shall stand while crowns and laurels fail,
And Time strews men like leaves upon the gale.

Proud land, to give such honored men their graves!
Long as thy shore the broad Pacific laves
Or soars to heaven Mount Shasta's brow of awe
(Like that "white throne" and vast th' Evangel saw),
Shall thy most rare and golden name be crowned
With all that glory gives, the world around!
Still shall the nations visit thee from far,
(With Hesper deemed a not unequal star;)
Still shalt thou lavish, pour thy treasures forth,
Enriching all from thy exhaustless worth;
Still shall thy sons be brave, thy daughters fair,
And Art and Science breathe thy purer air.

MY LOST LOVE.

I saw her when my heart was young,
   And she was beautiful and fair,
With silver music on her tongue,
   And golden glory in her hair;
And all love's glances round her flung,
   And Eve's first sweetness in her air.

I saw her 'mid the giddy throng
   My bosom filled with wild romance;
T'was she who sang the sweetest song,
   And she the stateliest in the dance..
Oh, could her heart to me belong,
   Her kisses warm my soul entrance!

I saw her by the wildwood stream,
   Where swung the lilies tall and pale,
And roses kissed the sunny beam,
   And by their blushes told the tale—
And rose and lily (love the theme)
   Upon her check did grow and fail.

"That rose's image in the wave,"
   She said, "how sweet, reflected there!
Yet one rude gale it cannot brave,
   But scattered all its beauties are."
"Its perfume still the flower shall save
   Which lives on shore, and bless the air."

"It too shall pass," she sadly said.
   I could not reason with her mood,
But felt the shadow of her dread
   E'en in that summer solitude.
Oh, Heaven, shelter that dear head,
   Though flowers may die in this lone wood!

I saw her when the dawning Day
   Was sculpturing from the silent night,
Her white and stainless form ; each ray
   Revealed new raptures to my sight,
And, as the darkness fell away,
   My arms enfolded all delight.

I saw her in another's arms!
   Oh, Death, within thy cold embrace.
The lily's bloom, the rose's charms
   Affrighted from that fairest face.
Oh, cruel is the fate which harms
   What God himself can ne'er replace.

I saw her next-alas, no more!
   How desolate a soul can be!
I wandered to the streamlet's shore,
   No rose nor lily could I see;
Yet fell a voice: "To thee no more
   I come, but thou shalt come to me."

POEM. [9]

ALL hail, the fairest, greatest, best of days!
With heaving hearts, and tongues attuned to praise.
Behold, what thousands at thy coming throng,
With bannered pomp, with eloquence and song.
Upon her path impulsive bounds the earth,
As conscious of her deed of grandest birth;
And Time's Recorder, standing in the sun,
To count the orbic periods as they run,

---

[9]   Delivered at San Francisco, July 4th, 1861.

Re-notes the chiefest hour of all the age,
And finds new glory on his blazing page.
Oh, well this day may throbbing bosoms beat,
And fervent spirits feel divinest heat,
And young and old, with willing steps and free,
And voices glad as waves of summery sea,
Come forth from cottage and from hail, to fling
On Freedom's shrine the tributes that they bring!

Well might the theme the meanest muse inspire,
To sweep the willing chords with hand of fire,
For, burning in the firmament of fame,
Each name renowned pours down its flood of flame,
And deeds come crowding in the path of years,
Till all the Past in one grand scene appears;
And standing midst the wondrous days of old,
We seem, with unvailed vision to behold
What Kings with trembling and with awe surveyed,
The deep foundations of an empire laid.
With Adams and with Washington we see
The growing of the shadowed prophecy,
And watch, elate, the pillared structure rise,
Till, crowned with stars, and domed amid the skies,
It fronts the Nations in its strength and, lo!
Amidst the rapture of the hour aglow,
From yonder far-seen Heaven's supremest heights
Descendeth IMMORTALITY, and writes
Her name upon its constellated brow!
Long years, or bright or dark that tower has stood—
Full many a siege has braved of fire and flood;
Contending factions sweeping at its base at will,
The storms have cleared and left it glorious still.
Through night and darkness has its beacon light
Still shone upon the nation's wondering sight;
And when they looked to see its proud dome bend,
And midst the blackening gloom and wreck descend,

It rose, emerging from the tempest's shock,
Like Chimborazo's condor-nesting rock!

But in our dome the eagle builds its nest,
And with our banner flies with armored breast;
Yet, crawling round those pillars white, we've seen
Beneath his perch, those meaner things unclean;
That hissing wind where demigods have trod!
They've slimed Mount Vernon's consecrated sod.
In all the nation's highways still we meet
Their coiling shapes, and in the august seat,
Where sat a Washington, but late we found
The meanest reptile of them all inwound.
But now these slimier things their tasks have done,
And in their stead comes forth the monster one,
Their many-headed sire ! Yea, Treason rears
Aloft his snaky front, and impious, dares
The high and holy place, where sits enthroned
Our country's Genius, with her armies zoned.
Black rolls the cloud o'er friend and foe alike—
But whom, whom shall the bolts of vengeance strike?
Methinks the starry banner that had braved
The regal mistress of the deep, has waved
Where Cortez' banners soared; with victory blest,
Has rippled in the breezes of the west;
In northern hurricane has tost, and known
But triumph in its march from zone to zone,
Shall never sink before you rebel crew—
Shall never bow, vile traitors, unto you!

Ah, would those tongues could speak which now are dumb!
For, lo! the evil days have on us come,
And heroes, patriots stand appalled to see
In hands untried the nation's destiny.
Good men and true there are-strong men and bold;
But not, oh, not the mighty men of old!

'Twas not till Jackson's heart was dust; till Day
To Night had given the electric brain of Clay;
Till God-like Webster's all imperial mind,
From its vast sphere of living light declined,
That Treason, scourged into his den, did dare
Again come forth to foul the shrinking air,
And blot the face of Freedom's soil with births
That Hell shall own too monstrous for the earth's.
And he who stood those men of strength beside,
In heart and brain and breadth of soul allied,
The statesman of a younger time, but tried
In days his elders might have shrunk to see—
The gallant, glorious Douglas, where is he?
The hosts that rallied to his battle cry,
And deemed such power was never made to die,
Now weep above the spot whose sods enfold
The man of might this orb shall seldom mould.
He died too soon, but other souls sublime
Shall spring perchance, from out this troublous time.
And, seizing from each silent chieftain's grave
The drooping, mourning standards of the brave,
Their folds unfurl and bear them to the field
Where free-born patriots die but never yield.

God of our fathers, grant that such there be!
And round them pour the millions of the free.
Let voice to voice, and hand to hand, and soul
To soul, give answer, and combine, as roll
The waves unto the marching winds that sweep
Cloud-bannered, thunder-armed, upon the deep.
In peace or war still let our Nation stand—
Fair Liberty still haunt her native land,
And long, long after we have sunk to dust,
And crowns and kingdoms failed, as fail they must,
And Treason, spreading wide its serpent toils
Has died, self-stung in its own coils—

This frame gigantic of our Nation's might,
Shall loom upon the world's enraptured sight,
Still bearing on its broad, majestic brow,
ESTO PERPETUA -Eternal be, as now.

THE "SINGING SPIRIT." [10]

WITHIN the forest's depths I wandered once
    And sweetest warbling music heard—
Methought it were the water-sprite at first,
    And then some lonely singing bird!
And still the music in its softness rose
    And fell upon my heart like light,
Which from its dreary realm dispelled
    Pale Sadness, with her robe of night.

The shadows left my sobered, pensive brow,
    My soul uprising freshen'd seemed,
And every thing I gazed upon as now,
    Took hues of which so oft I've dreamed!
I glanced from stem to stem and bough to bough,
    To catch the little warbler's form,
To see what shape embodied thus,
    And made suspense so fine a charm!

I gazed, but could not see. The music thrilled
    Along my beings in most strings,
Till melody had all my bosom filled,
    And overrun its secret springs.
The tear stood trembling in my eye, and hushed
    To feeling's pause was every breath—
The tones became so low, that I
    Half deemed them warning me of death.

---

[10]   A Poem addressed to Miss A. A. B.

And yet there was no dread-I thought, how meet
   'Neath such a dirge to sink and die!
While viewless o'er was heard that harp, how sweet
   To close the dim and fading eye!
Then rose the lifted voice to sudden power,
   And yet not harsh, but rich and deep
As is the feeling of the soul
   When mighty thoughts our natures sweep.

Ah me, 'T were vain with language to describe
   The wild sensations of my breast;
Till I some angel's brightest pen can bribe,
   That spirit-thrill must be supprest!
Still floated round those ever changing notes,
   Now with a burst, and now a moan,
And I thought in Northern Land
   I'd heard and treasured such a tone!

The music died at last, as sweetest things
   Must die!—and homeward I returned.
But often in my lonely wanderings
   Once more to hear that voice I yearned;
Then grieving that I heard it not, I named
   It in the soul it had enthralled.
And ever after to myself
   The "Singing Spirit" it was called.

DO I LOVE THEE?

If I could love my God as well,
   'T would build for me a heavenly throne;
But, when I raise my eyes to HIM,
   I see thy own sweet form alone;

And, dreaming of the harps of Heaven,
  I hear but thy melodious tone.

Thou stealest upon me silently,
  And tak'st possession of my heart,
And ere my breast can question aught,
  I find thee of myself a part—
Commingling with my blood and soul,
  My own life's purer life thou art!

Oft in yen mountain's woodiest scene
  I dream of some sweet spirit-bride,
So beautiful in mental grace,
  She seems Creation's joy and pride;
And, when I hear her footsteps near,
  I see thy image by my side.

Oh, many a dream I've had, sweet one,
  And thou hast been the living light
Which still hath lit my fancy's realm,
  And beautified the lonely night—
The night whose varying shapes assumed
  The witching smile and image bright.

At times, when fever pains my brow,
  A fair-faced, blue-eyed angel bends
Above my tortured form, and smiles
  So sweetly on me that it lends
A beauty unto pain, and makes
  Me rank disease among my friends.

How have I thrilled, as to my lips
  Her own have tenderly been prest,
And drank the life of her warm heart
  And love immortal from her breast—
But drained it not, for still it rose
  A fountain pure and ever blest.

A SCENE ALONG THE RIO DE LAS PLUMAS.

With solemn step I trace
A dark and dismal place,
Where moss with trailing ends,
From heavy boughs depends;
Where day resembles night,
And birds of sullen flight
Pierce darkness with their screams;
Where slow and sluggish streams
Crawl through the sleeping woods
And weirdful solitudes.
In dreamy languor bound,
Upon their slimy breast
The lolling lilies rest,
And from their depths profound
Strange things, with staring eyes
And uncouth limbs, arise—
A moment gaze with mute surprise
Then sink adown like lead,
And seek their oozy bed.

What looks a spirit there,
Snow-white upon the air,
And hov'ring over these
Deep pools and drooping trees,
As if some heavenly sprite
Had come from Day to Night,
Is but the crane that feeds,
When hungered 'mong the reeds;
Or sloughs, flag-margined, wades,
Meandering 'neath the shades,
And makes his vulgar dish
Of creeping things and fish.

Yon ermined owl that flits
Through dusky leaves, or sits
In somber silence now
On yonder ivyed bough,
And looks a druid priest—
No higher thoughts inspire
Than lowest wants require,
As how to make his feast,
When lurking mouse or bird
Hath from its covert stirred.

Those flaming eyes awake
In yonder thorny brake,
Which dilate as I pass,
Illumining the grass
And lighting darksome ground,
Are not from that profound,
Where cries of woe resound
And Dante's damned abound,
Nor yet the wandering ghouls,—
The dread of dead men's souls,—
(Because their flesh he craves,
And digs it from their graves),
But orbs of sinuous snake
Who from the neighboring lake
Or vapor-breeding bog,
His victim soon shall take—
Some luckless dozing frog.
Nor will thy lither shape,
Thou rodent sly escape,
If once thine eye hath caught
The fire within that head,
From venomed sources fed,
With fascination fraught.

A SCENE ALONG THE RIO DE LAS PLUMAS

I reach a dimmer nook,
And warily I look,
For where yon night-shades grow
And baneful blossoms blow,
Beneath the toadstools, well
I know ill-creatures dwell—
Tarantula, whose bite
Would strongest heart affright;
The stinging centipede,
Whose hundred-footed speed,
And hundred arm-ed feet
Bring death and danger fleet,
That, with Briarean clasp,
The fated victim grasp,
And scorpion, single-stinged,
Fabled erst as winged,
And still reported wide,
If pressed, a suicide.

And here I see—but lo!
I can no further go,
For what's this hum I hear
Which fills the atmosphere,
And drums the tingling car
Till, half distraught, I reel?
I heard, but now I feel!
Good sakes, what winged forms!
What singing, dizzing swarms!
Ten thousand needles flamed
Could not with them be named.

THE STILL SMALL VOICE.

ALAS, how every thing will borrow
Hues, tones, and bitterness from sorrow!
   If evening comes with softened ray
   To close the eye of dying day;
If morning ushers in the morrow
   With dew-drops sprinkled on its way,
'Tis all the same; a voice is whispering from the Past—
"Too late! too late! the doom is set, the die is cast!"

If through the woods my footsteps roam,
Where always they do feel at home,
   And wandering leisurely I trace
   Each streamlet to its rising place,
To hear its music, see its foam,
   No tide of sound, no shape of grace
Can hush that solemn voice, that whispering from the Past—
"Too late I too late! the doom is set, the die is cast!"

If o'er some well-loved page I bend
In converse deep as with a friend
   Whose kindly tones I love to hear,
   That lowly sound will reach. my ear,
And sadly with my feelings blend
   As sigh with sigh and tear with tear!
The mighty thoughts I read all fade before the Past,
Which cries "too late! the doom is set, the die is cast!"

Oh, never hushed that voice will be!
As sadly as the mournful sea,
   Where savage silent shores it laves,
   And darkness dwells upon its waves,
Do sound its low-breathed tones to me!

The peace my bosom often craves,
Will linger but a moment's space—it flies the Past,
Whose voice yet cries "the doom is set, the die is cast!"

   A raven-thought is darkly set
     Upon my brow—where shades are met
       Of grief, of pain, of toil, and care—
       The raven-thought of stern despair!
   Oh, wherefore are my eyelids wet,
     While birds make music on the air?
No ear but mine can catch the breathings of the Past,
"Too late! too late I the doom is set, the die is cast!"

   Adieu, sweet scenes of other days;
     Ye sleep within the past, like rays
       Of moonlight on a silent lake.
       'Tis not within my power to wake
     Your slumbers with these feeble lays;
       I can but feel my bosom quake
To hear the low but awful fiat of the Past—
"Too late! too late! the doom is set, the die is cast!"

EYES.

I SING of eyes, of woman's eyes,
   A theme from earliest ages sung,
But which, till all of nature dies,
   Shall ever hid the harp be strung.

There is the eye of sober gray;
   Which seems to shadow forth regret,
As if the spirit mourned alway
   Its starry hopes forever set.

There is the eye of hazel bright,
   Which wins and dazzles where it falls,
Reviving with its showers of light
   The happy bosom it enthralls.

There is the eye of tender blue,
   Soft as the heaven at set of sun,
Which many deem is ever true,
   And smiles on all but speaks to one.

There is the eye of darker hue,
   Which rivals Midnight on her throne;
Now softly bright as streams that through
   The shady forests wander lone;

Now like a cloud that hides from sight
   The beauty of the rolling spheres,
And flashes far with angry light,
   Or sinking downwards melts to tears.

As sages loved in ancient days
   To read the heavens when darkness fell,
So on those orbs of black we gaze,
   And feel our inmost bosoms swell.

As lovely as the worlds that lie
   Reposing in the Nights embrace,
Is the soft meaning of that eye,
   And deeper than the depths of space!

I cease—for all description's vain;
   Let each one choose the eye he likes,
That melts the heart or soothes the brain,
   Or like the dreaded lightning strikes;

But as for me, I love those eyes,
   No matter what their hues may be,
To which the hearts warm feelings rise
   In overflowing love to me.

Alternate fount of light and tears,
   Their smiles are sweet, their sadness too,
And I could joy or grieve for years,
   As those fond eyes might bid me do!

POEM.[11]

HAIL to the Plow! for naught shall take its place,
he first, great civilizer of the race!
Still honored by the wisest and the best
In every age where'er its power has blest!
For long before the Mantuan bard had sung
His Georgics in the grand old Roman tongue,
Or deified Triptolemus, revealed
The mysteries in Ceres breast concealed;
Or Egypt's kings their pyramids upreared,
To brave old Time and dark Oblivion feared;
Or e'er old China's wall stupendous rose
Long ages since, 'gainst barbarous Tartar foes;
Or e'er the Parsee worshiper of fire
His altars lit where Elbrooz heights aspire;
Or Afric Carthage built grim Moloch's throne,
Or Ninevah arose, or Babylon,
The plow, presager of the Arts, was known!

---

[11]   Delivered before the Agricultural, Horticultural, and Mechanic's Society of the Northern District of California, on Wednesday Evening, August 5th, 1860.

Though rude of form, yet in its furrowed track
Fair Plenty trode and paid swart Labor back
Ten-fold his toil; for in those days, as now,
The Earth was kind to him who drave the plow.

With Agriculture sprang whate'er in Art
Has raised the mind or purified the heart—
Whate'er in Science hath exalted man.
And glorified him since the world began;
And still to Agriculture do we trace
The first faint gleam of progress in the race.

The Nations justly vaunted now and great—
Old days beheld them in the hunter state,
When clad in skins, and quivers on their backs,
They followed on the wild deer's bounding tracks;
Or sought, through wood and brake and fen,
The fierce and gnashing boar within his den;
Or earned a slim subsistence by the shore
Of lakes and rivers with their scaly store.
Tanned by the sun and dew, their beaten forms
Still harder fired in wintry winds and storms;
Nor homes had they save where they nightly found
Chance lodging on the bare, ungrateful ground.
Small share was here, I ween, of luxury,
Nor downy couch, nor cushioned seat had they—
Smile not-such were our own rude ancestry!
Next came the pastoral days, when men less roved,
But pitched their camps by pleasant springs, nor moved
Till pastures failed or rival flocks their bounds
Did press, intrusive on their chosen grounds.
Still 'Twas a roving life, surrounded too
By foes and daily dangers not a few,
For force 'gainst force those days prevailed, and laws
Were none, and each man's arm made good his cause.

But came in turn the third and better state,
With cheering omens of a higher fate.
Then, did the restless Nomad cease to roam—
His hardships o'er, he found at last his home.
From year to year he still improved his land,
Till beautiful it grew beneath his hand,
And laden vine and bleating flocks increase,
And waving fields gave all his days to peace.
Few fears alarmed him, for he knew the soil
Would aye repay with generous yield his toil.
Around him grew, with hope and joy elate,
His children fair that crowned his blest estate.
And near him soon new fields and cots were seen
Where late the brooding wilderness had been;
Then grew up mutual interests and needs,
And all that such community succeeds.
Against the still untamed and savage man
The armed alliance of the few began;
And soon Society on mutual wants arose,
With peace at home and guards against its foes.
New wants still with the social fabric grew,
And needful laws as complicate as new.
Thus government was formed, and every man
Was safe and happy in the general plan.
Secure in property and life, each wrought
In his own way and ends congenial sought
Thus fixed in homes, could be no spoiler's prey,
Each gave his sep'rate faculties free play;
And soon Invention various needs supplied
And luxuries to hardier times denied.
Meantime like states in other lands had grown,
With laws, inventions, products of their own,
What lacked one clime another clime possest,
And each could still contribute to the rest.
Thus Commerce rose, and, stimulating art,
Gave impulse to Invention and new start

To all improvements that a Nation raise
And make a people's glory, wealth and praise.
Upgrew from rude beginnings like to these
Those states renowned along the Tuscan seas,
And she who sat by Tiber's yellow tide
In pomp of riches and imperial pride.
Thus sprang those capitals of Eastern lands,
Long buried in the desert's shifting sands,
Whose fallen, rescued monuments avow,
In sculptured yoke and hieroglyphic plow,
Their debt to agricultural toil. They fell—
As fell the grand old Rome—because too well
They loved the bannered pomp of conquering war,
Neglecting arts of peace more glorious far,
While fought the soldier at a despot's will,.
The rusting plow within the field stood still,
And hosts, returning from a vanquished land,
Spread vice and luxury on every hand.
For every soldier on the tented plain
One less to prune the vine and sow the grain—
And armies counted by the million leave
Broad fields to waste that years will not retrieve.

As on the other continent on this
With Agriculture came true happiness,
And man advanced by sure and slow degrees
From savage toil and strife to rest and ease.
As England was in Alfred's time (The Great),
So civilized was Montezuma's state,
And burning bright his fair and peaceful star,
When Cortez came with red right hand of war.
Let truth impartial say, if happier now
Is that historic land, broad Mexico,
Than when all greenly spread the cultured plain,
And waved the far Cordilleras with grain,
And rolled the deep canals, with streams that blest

POEM

A thousand homes in Eden beauty drest,
And all the realm from mountain slope to main,
Was fair Montezuma's golden reign?
Was art, that built those cities vast, less art,
Because of Aztec genius 'Twas a part?
Was patient toil, that led thro' channels deep,
And aqueducts, and 'long the rocky steep,.
The streams a thousand fertile fields supplied,
Less toil, because no white man's arm was tried?
Were peace and plenty but the Spaniard's right?
The Aztec *barbarous* because not *white*?

As much and more the arts of peace had done
For Peru's realm,—soft children of the Sun.
For, long before the white man's foot had pressed,
Or north or south, the Cont'nent of the West,
The Inca's sway had civilized Peru—
A land as happy as the world e'er knew!
'Twas not her temples blazing rich with gold,
And showering light from starry gems untold;
Her palaces of gorgeous pomp and pride,
Where sat her rich-robed Incas deified
Her golden statues and her carvings rare
Of bird and reptile on the burnished ware,
That made the glory of her tranquil state,
And almost won for her the title "great"!
It was her homes, by many a winding rill,
By rivers wide, in vale, on terraced hill,
Where grew the waving corn, or wand'ering fed
The fleecy flocks by watchful shepherds led;
Her pleasant cots, where sheltered from the sun,
Peruvian wives and damsels sat and spun,
Or wove their plumaged pictures-from the wings
Of tropic birds-of rare and beauteous things,
Or through the loom's ingenious workings fast
The Alpacca's fleece with skillful fingers passed.

Let paler nations vaunt themselves and praise
Their slow advancement from the savage days;
If government is wisest that's designed
For good of greatest number of the kind,
Methinks no just philosophy will scan
With scornful eyes the Peru Indian's plan—
A policy which gave with equal hand
To each his due proportion of the land,
And each his share of what the general toil
Produced from manufacture or the soil..
As labor was enjoined on all, so none
Could suffer when the seasoned work was done.
As all, too, labored duly for the State,
If sickness fell or any evil fate,
The State provided, not as charity
But right, for him whose former industry,
Still looking to the common weal in this,
Had swelled her coffers and her granaries.
In all the realm no subject could be poor,
But peace and plenty sat at each man's door.
No happier lot the poet's dream can find,
Nor Art nor Science reach for human kind;
Not all the Old World's civilization vast,
Nor yet our own, the grandest and the last,
To that one culminating point has come—
To give each man a competence and home.

Thus in her own rude way' our muse has shown
How man in all that blesses him has grown
With Agriculture and the arts of peace,
And how with them these blessings still increase—
The mind and heart still growing with the growth
Of that which first gave training unto both.
For while the genius of the plow and spade
Improvement still on willing nature made—
The cultured flower expanding. into size

Unknown before and tinct with richer dyes,
New forms assuming from the fecund dust
Not left to chance and to the zephyr's trust,
But, like with unlike pollen mixed, till strange
Creations bloomed and wonder marked the change;
The human soul, the Man, expanded too,
And found in realms of thought the strange and new.

A pleasant task were ours, could we so grace
Our pen, the history of the plow to trace—
Its allied helps of Science and the Arts,
And all that to its reign new strength imparts;
How in the Roman and the Grecian sway
It made the glory of their proudest day;
How it for ages knew but small regard,
When warriors fought and sang the warrior bard;
How after times sought knowledge that was hid
In monkish cells the mountain rocks amid,
And drew from monasterial lore and skill
The ancient art the fruitful earth to till;
How pruning, grafting came; how science found
New modes to fertilize the failing ground—
Ammonia's properties, the silicates,
The strength of guano, phosphates, and their mates,
And whatsoever else may give the earth
Its fecund power and swelling joy of birth;
And how Improvement with the years kept pace,
And Agriculture blest the human race.

But now we turn, a not ungrateful theme,
To realize the El Dorado dream
In that one land which all that dream fulfills—
The land whose name the world's heart thrills—
Our own unequaled, Golden State! the clime
Of wonder, cynosure of modern time!
What silver word, what golden line can say

The half its worth, its matchless wealth portray?
If soars the muse along her mountain chains
Where Grandeur, snow-crowned, rocky-girdled reigns;
Or glides adown her golden-sanded streams;
Or with the miner plunges deep where gleams,
Mysterious in the hill's eternal night,
The ore revealed by dimly-flickering light;
Or seeks along the barren, ghostly coast,
The caverned realms where, in black basins tost,
The springs of bitumen boil up to sight;
Or wings to Napa's weirdful land her flight,
Where, bursting forth from many a fissured rock,
With hot but healing breath and angry shock,
The imprisoned demon of the earth makes known
His fearful presence in the under-zone;
Or penetrates where Labor seeks its gains
In Santa Clara's quick, mercurial veins;
Or Shasta's treasure-laden ground explores,
Her springs of salt, her marble, and her ores;
Or scans in Calaveras' mammoth pride
The trunks three thousand winters have defied,
Where'er in all this sunset-land she flies,
New signs, new wonders meet her maz-ed eyes.

But California's glory is not told
By wealth of resource like to this-her gold,
Her hidden riches in the earth, her stores
Of precious undeveloped things, her ores,
Her quarries vast, her springs medicinal—
Beyond all these and far surpassing all
Akin to these, her Agriculture stands,
The pride of earth, the envy of all lands!
Prolific soil! within itself it yields
Of every clime the fruits. Its smiling fields
The tasseled maize affords; the waving wheat,
Hemp, rice ; the jointed cane with essence sweet;

The many-seeded fig; its tropic mate;
The oily olive, tamarind, and date;
The pear and peach; the grape, as rare and fine
In all that gilds the immemorial vine,
As ever grew in shepherd days of peace,
In native beauty on the hills of Greece—
Or wild in woods that skirt the Arabian sea
The wandering savage fed with bounty free—
Or in Italia's purpled vales did hang
To lips as ripe, that I-brace kissed and sang.
Here grow those garden monsters that surprise
Like miracles our scarce-believing eyes,
Reminding us of that Titanic age
Recorded in the geologic page,
When shrubs were trees, and plants that now in lines
Our gardens green, had dwarfed Norwegian pines.
Of .that same soil, which thus prolific threw
Those giants forth, when yet the world was new,
Our soil partakes. And thus we leave behind
All climes and lands, and wonder-strike mankind.
Fair Land! but fairer yet shall be—for still
Shall Industry her hills and valleys till,
And Agriculture write on many a spot
Her name in verdure, where before 'Twas not.
As Franklin his, when wondering rustics saw
A miracle in Nature's simplest law.

'Tis Irrigation, wondrous art, though old,
With aids of modern science manifold,
Shall work the magic change we yet shall see,
When all the desert lands shall cultured be;
When from the Sacramento's margin green,
Or tule borders of the San Joaquin,
To eastern peaks, whose curving line of show
Like some white arm of beauty all aglow
With love, enwreaths the nestling hills below;

From yonder western slopes that lave
Their feet within the blue Pacific's wave
To woods infringing on the arid plain
That heated ripples to the mountain chain;
From Northern heights of rugged Siskiyou
Whose vales abysmal hide from view,
To where the smoothly shaven waters ply
In sheltered San Diego's tranquil bay;
The land shall blossom with its edens fair,
The fruitful hills make fragrant all the air,
And breezy valleys wave their yellow hair.
For, mark you, Art, with Science aid, shall make
Spots fertile which the ignorant forsake;
And all that weary waste of hazy heat,
O'er which the heron's lonely wing doth beat
In effort vain some moistured spot to find
Shall prove to man's enlightened labor kind.
The hidden fountains of the earth shall rise,
And mock with coolness all the brazen skies;
The piercing steel shall strike the secret vein
That, bursting forth, shall fertilize the plain.
And soon where late no blade or leaf was seen
Shall orchards bloom and waving fields be green.
Oh Land of Beauty! why the theme prolong?
Like that delicious isle of Indian song,
Which, o'er the waters gliding, fled pursuit,
Thou hast all gems, all wealth, all golden fruit,
And, far more blest than Indian dreamers were,
We lose thee not, a vision of the air!

THE ARKANSAW ROOT DOCTOR.[12]

ON Osage Creek, in Arkansaw, amid
The wild-browed hills there stands a cabid hid;
The boards are shattered badly on the roof;
And when it rains it is not water-proof;
The wooden chimney totters to one side,
As though a posture straight it did deride;
The puncheon floor's uneven and so rough
A naked foot to stand it should be tough;
The door upon its hinge half hangs, and creaks
Most dolefully when shut!

Close by there breaks
From out a gently rising hill so pure
A stream, some madness of the brain 'T would cure;
Below't through which this pure stream runs, a lot
There is, fenced round—a green and grassy spot,
Whose verdure 's all the nourishment that grows
For one old horse, who well that pasture knows.
Through many a long and slowly rolling year
That old gray horse has fed, a MUSARD here!
Bereft of sight, he seems reflecting sad
On all the joys his buoyant colt-hood had;
But, like some stoic, weather-beaten sage,
He seems resigned to all the griefs of age!
His owner dwells within that cabin rude,
A man of forty, fond of solitude.
From manhood's earliest years his searching mind
Has striven hard a secret truth to find;
The face of herbal nature he 's perused,
On all the properties of plants has mused;
No mountain's been too savage or too high
For him—he'd scale it, if it touched the sky!

---

[12] A true sketch.

No glen has been too dark—his prying look,
That's ever keen, will no denial brook,
When searching for that herb, whose root shall save
The well from pain, the dying from the grave!
A noble work on earth he dreams is his:
To find the source, the ROOT of happiness!
The lore of letters he has never known—
He claims the book of "natur" as his own!
He deems the knowledge which is learned in schools
But fitted for a polished pack of fools;
His mind ne'er soars above the ground; the earth
Contains beneath its surface all that's worth,
In his idea, the search of man, Poor fool!
He's wise because he never went to school!

In searching for the healing root desired,
He's found some other ones for health required,
And, having in slight mixing with his kind,
Revealed by chance the treasures of his mind,
His neighbors onewhile kept him much engaged—
For fevers dread on Osage frequent raged.
On's old gray horse, the country up and down,
Was seen each day the noted Doctor Brown;
A bunch of roots was to his saddle tied,
Another bundle hanging at his side;
He ministered, with tender hand and care,
To those who pale on life's last limits were;
He smoothed the pillow for the feverish head—
He bathed—he purged—he sweated—and he bled!
But Death forever triumphed o'er his art,
And left the good, kind doctor sick at heart.
So frequent did the deaths become where he
Was sent, himself became a Malady;
And when the good Root-finder came to save,
He seemed to patients, Herald of the Grave!
At last no one in Dr. Brown believed—

THE ARKANSAW ROOT DOCTOR

Much wronged by men's opinions he conceived
Himself and from that day, henceforth, retired
To find the long-sought root so much desired.

One faithful pupil has he, named Bill Skid,
Who tracks him everywhere and does as bid;
These two (and that old horse to bear the roots),
Not caring for the busy world and its pursuits,
Each day are traveling o'er the hills around,
With anxious gaze bent down upon the ground,
Intent to see some leaf of different size
Or hue, reveal itself unto their eyes.
They stop at intervals, and dig amain—
Then breaks the Doctor into raptured strain,
Describing to Bill Skid's wondering soul
The mighty mystery of art:

"The whole
Secret of medicine is this-To SWEAT.
If in our sarching we kin get
A yarb that'll do this bizness, Bill,
No sickness know'd of then will kill!
The reason so many people dies,
Is caze the Doctors tells them lies—
If they'd tell 'em to always sweat
As much as they kin, and to eat
Nothing that'll hander it, folks would
Live as long agin! It's so good
To sweat, I'd advise you to let
No chance pass. To live long. JIST SWEAT."

One day in their accustomed rounds they came
Upon a plant with blossom red as flame—
They hailed it with delight-both held their hands
In silence for awhile—Bill waits commands—
The Doctor bade him dig. He dug. The root

Was large, and of a color brown as soot;
"Taste it, Bill," says Dr. Brown; "God! no," says Bill,
"I'm feered it mought have the defect to kill—
Lessen you had yer Low-Billy along?"
"I've got it." They both taste. The root was strong
And bitter as could be. Directly, pains
Began to seize them—rueful throes and strains!
The doctor searched his pockets for the vial
Of Lobelia which he kept for the trial
Of experiments with herbs—but 'Twas gone!
At this discovery both were headlong thrown—
They fell upon the ground in agony;
Each crying lustily: "Oh God!" "Oh me!"
The med'cine worked them savagely. One hour
They rolled upon the hill-side—still with power
The root was operating, and no peace
To Dr. Brown and Skid! It would not cease,
But kept their stomachs in ferment extreme,
As though they were hot engines full of steam;
Until, exhausted with the torment, they
All motionless, outstretched, at full length lay!
When they uprose at last, they both were white
As is a sheeted ghost late in the night;
Their limbs were trembling; downward rolled the sweat;
Says Bill, "Well, that's the toughest med'cine yet!"
"God I yes," replied the doctor, panting loud,
"The sweat rolls down like water from a cloud—
I b'lieve in this-this is *the* yarb at last!
A root that sweats a fellow so *d—d* fast
Must be the one I 'in sarching for! Hoo-ray!
The greatest yarb on airth I've found to-day!"

And now these students of the healing art
Are seen each morn at dawn of day to start,
With their old, gray horse, into the woods;

Take good care to have Lobelia stowed away
In deer-skin saddle-bags, lest once again
Some bold experiment may cause them pain;
They gather in particular the herb
Which did their inward organs so disturb,
Believing in the noblest gift of earth,
And more than all Time's lettered learning worth.

 Two such industrious men are nowhere seen:
They're martyrs to the cause they're busied in;
For constant trial of some new plant doth
Exercise so much their systems both,
That they are pale and withered in the face,
And their forms have lost all natural grace!
They seem the skeletons of men entombed,
Who have by some convulsion been exhumed,
Allowed to journey 'midst the human race,
To show the terrors of a darker place!

 So let them journey on-so let them weave
The mighty wonders dying they shall leave;
Yes, let them labor, like their old horse, blind,
And hope by digging roots to save mankind!

THE MAIDEN'S FORTUNE.

I'm Queen of the Gipsies-yon fate-bearing star
Has guided my steps to this region afar;
And I with my people thus westward shall roam,
Till Egypt receives our old, primal home.
Yet many a fortune of peace or of strife
Shall vary the scenes of our wandering life,
Ere the land of our fathers, dusk land of the Nile,
Shall welcome us back, with its warm, sunny smile;

From my tent in the woods, where, all the long day,
The wind-sifted leaves with these winds are at play,
And the mountain-born streamlets as musical roll
As the answering gush of sweet thoughts in the soul;
From my tent in the woods, with its mossy-green seat,
The birds in the branches, the blooms at my feet,
And every thing round me as happy as they,
I come to thy presence, thou beautiful May!

No gifts can I bring thee of tangible show;
But Fate and the stars 'Tis my province to know,
And these shall reveal me the dark or the bright
Of thy life and thy fortunes—I'll read them to-night.
Ah, well do I see in the horoscoped years
The shadows of sorrows, the traces of tears!
What then? Is the story so soon to be told—
A life of brief date, with its griefs manifold!

Not so, for I view in this mystical sign,
Refigured the joys on the pathway to shine.
As the mists of the morning, low draping the hills,
Thy tears shall be transient, as transient their ills.
Adown a long path of the fortunate years,
What form do I see which so lovely appears?
Like thine, if to womanhood regally grown,
A vision of beauty, but she walks not alone!
Erect in his manhood, of manhood the pride,
A being to worship behold at her side.
His smile is the sunshine that brightens her brow,
Her bosom with blisses is rich and aglow.
Now fade they in dimness of distance to sight,
But the path still before them is beaming with light.
And now they are swallowed in radiance new-born,
Like birds that are lost in the gold of the morn.

RANDOM THOUGHTS OF HER.

I GAZE into her eyes—their tender light,
And strong, illumes my spirit's darkest night,
And pours rich glory on me as a star
Which brings its silver luster from afar.

Sweet thoughts and beautiful within me burn,
And heaven I see what way soe'er I turn;
In borrowed radiance of her soulful glance
All things grow tenfold lovely and entrance.

I touch her willing hand—as gentle dove
It rests within my own, in trusting love;
And yet it moves me with a power so deep,
My heart is flame, and all my pulses leap.

I breathe her name unto the flowers: they bloom
With rarer hues, and shed more rich perfume!
The skylark hears it, as he floats along,
And adds new sweetness to his morning song.

Oh magic name! deep graven on my heart,
And, as its owner, of myself a part!
It hath in all my daily thoughts a share,
And forms the burden of my nightly prayer!

OTHER POEMS

TO A****.

I would not give one smile of thine,
For all the names renowned in story—
I'd rather press thy lips to mine,
Than wear their richest wreath of glory!

I would not take a monarch's crown
For thy sweet voice, like dews distilling—
I'd throw the cumbrous burden down,
To meet thy warm embraces thrilling!

The golden sun, if I could coin—
The silver moon and stars—at pleasure,
My soul and heart with thine to join,
I'd spurn as trash that heap of treasure!

For thee, alas! thy winning ways,
I'd rend the ties of friend or brother,
And give one half of all my days,
If thou would'st love me thro' the other.

FAR IN A LONELY WOOD. [13]

Far in a lonely wood I wandered once,
Where warbling birds of melancholy wing
And music sad rehearsed their melancholy songs.
All else was silent save the whispering leaves
Strewn by autumnal winds, or here and there
A stream which ever poured a mournful sound
Amid those solitudes so dim, where shadows

---

[13] This untitled poem was signed "Yellow Bird," and dated "Osage, July 18, 1847. It was reprinted in the Arkansas Gazette, July 20, 1941.

Vast and tall, eternal threw their flickering
Darkness. Retrospection sadly turned my mind
To scenes now painted on the map of Time
Long past. And as I wandered on, I mused
On greatness fall'n, beauteous things destroyed;
When suddenly my footstep paused before
A mound of moss-grown earth. I wondered,
For a while, what mortal here had found
A resting place? But soon I minded me,
That many years agone a noble race
Had roamed these forest-wilds among and made
These mountain fastnesses rebound to shouts
Of liberty untamed, and happiness
That knew no bounds. I recollected now,
That, save but a few, they all had fled,
And, fleeing, left some bones behind; the only
Mark that this fair land was once their heritage.
By Nature's gift to her untutored sons.
Then thought I, "This must be the grave of one
Who ranked among the warriors of the
Wilderness!—And when he saw his country
Doomed, his tribe o'erthrown, and his strong arm
Grown weak before his pale-faced foes; and when
He knew the hour was come, in which his soul
Must leave the form it once had moved to noble
Deeds, and travel to the hunting-grounds, where erst
His fathers went, he here had dug his grave,
And singing wild his death-song to the wind,
Sunk down and died!"
Sleep on, dark warrior.
Whoe'er thou art! My hand shall not disturb
The slightest stem that takes its nutriment
From thee. The white man's share may plough some other
Mounds where Red men sleep, round which no mourner
Stands in watch to guard the relics of a friend;
But no rude step, and no rude hand shall e'en

Despoil the beauty of this silent spot;
Or sacrilegiously disturb the rest
Of one lone Indian form. Sleep on!
The storms that howled around thy head long,
Long ago, and tutored thy stern heart
To agony, have ceased. A thousand cities
Stand, where once thy nation's wigwam stood,
And numerous palaces of giant strength
Are floating down the streams when long ago
Thy bark was gliding. All is changed.
Then sleep thou on! Perchance this peace, denied
In life, within the lonely grave is found.

THE STILL SMALL VOICE.[14]

There is a voice more dear to me
Than man or woman's e'er could be—
A "still small voice" that cheers
The woes of these my darker years.

I hear it in the busy crowd,
Distinct, amid confusion loud;
And in the solemn midnight still,
When mem'ries sad my bosom fill.

I hear it midst the social glee,
A voice unheard by all but me;
And when my sudden trance is seen,
They wondering ask, what can it mean?

---

[14] This is a different poem than the one published in the 1868 edition. Signed "Yellow Bird," it was published in the Marysville (California) Herald on March 29, 1851.

The tones of woman once could cheer,
While woman yet to me was dear,
And sweet were all the dreams of youth,
As aught can be that wanteth truth!

How loved in early manhood's prime,
Ambition's clarion notes sublime!
How musical the tempest's roar,
"That lured to dash me on the shore!"

These tones, and more all beautiful,
That did my youthful spirit lull,
Or made my bosom Rapture's throne,
Have passed away, and left me lone.

And now that I can weep no more
The tears that gave relief of yore,
And now, that from my ruined heart
The forms that make me shudder, start;

I gaze above the world around,
And from the deeps of Heaven's profound,
A "still small voice" descends to me—
"Thou'rt sad, but I'll remember thee!"

As burns the life-light in me low,
And throws its ashes o'er my brow,
When all else flies, it speaks to me—
"Thou't doomed, but I'll remember thee!"

Then let my brow grow sadder yet,
And mountain-high still rise regret;
Enough for me the voice that cheers
The woes of these my darker years.

THE HUMBOLDT DESERT.

Who journeys o'er the desert now,
Where sinks engulfed the Humboldt river,
Arrested in its sudden flow,
But pouring in that depth forever.

As if the famished earth would drink
Adry the tributes of the mountains,
Yet wither on the water's brink,
And thirst for still unnumbered fountains.

Who journeys o'er that desert now
Shall see strange sights, I ween, and ghastly;
For he shall trace awearied, slow,
Across this waste extended vastly,

The steps of pilgrims westward bound,
Bound westward to the Land Pacific,
Where hoped for rest and peace are found,
And plenty waves her wand prolific.

Along this parched and dreary track,
Nor leaf, nor blade, nor shrub appeareth;
The sky above doth moisture lack,
And brazen glare the vision seareth;

Nor shadow, save the traveler's own,
Doth bless with coolness seeming only,
And save his muffled step alone
Or desert-bird's wild shriek and lonely,

No sound is heard—a realm of blight,
Of weird-like silence and a brightness
That maketh but a gloom of light,
Where glimmer shapes of spectral whiteness!

They are the bones that bleaching lie
Where fell the wearied beast o'er-driven,
And upward cast his dying eye,
As if in dumb appeal to heaven.

Far lengthening miles on miles they lie,
These sad memorials grim and hoary,
And every whitening heap we spy
Doth tell some way-worn pilgrim's story.

Hard by each skeleton there stand
The wheels it drew, or warped or shrunken,
And in the drifted, yielding sand
The yoke or rusted chain lies sunken.

Nor marvel we, if yonder peers,
From out some scooped-out grave and shallow,
A human head, which fleshless leers
With a look that doth the place unhallow.

Each annual pilgrimage hat strewn
These monuments unnamed, undated,
Till now were bone but piled on bone,
And heaped-up wrecks but congregated,

A pyramid would rise as vast
As one of those old tombs Egyptian,
Which speak from distant ages past
With time-worn, mystic, strange inscription.

But pass we these grim, mouldering things,
Decay shall claim as Time may order,

For, offspring of the mountain springs,
A river rims the desert border;

With margin green and beautiful,
And sparkling water silver-sounding,
And trees with zephyrs musical,
And answering birds with songs abounding,

And velvet flowers of thousand scents,
And clambering vines with blossoms crested;
Twas here the pilgrims pitched their tents,
And from their toilsome travel rested.

Oh sweet such rest to him who faints
Upon the journey long and weary!
And scenes like this the traveler paints,
While dying on the wayside weary.

Sad pilgrims o'er life's desert, *we*,
Our tedious journey onward ever;
But rest for us there yet shall be,
When camped upon the HEAVENLY RIVER.

SONG— SWEET INDIAN MAID.

Oh come with me, sweet Indian maid,
My light canoe is by the shore—
We'll ride the river's tide, my love,
And thou shalt charm the dripping oar.

Methinks thy hand could guide so well
The tiny vessel in its course;
The waves would smooth its crests to thee,
As I have done my spirit's force.

How calmly will we glide, my love,
Thro' moonlight drifting on the deep,
Or, loving yet the safer shore,
Beneath the fringing willows creep!

Again like some wild duck we'll skim,
And scarcely touch the water's face,
While silver gleams our way shall mark,
And circling lines of beauty trace.

And then the stars shall shine above
In harmony with those below,
And gazing up and looking down,
Give glance for glance, and glow for glow.

And all their light shall be our own,
Commingled with our souls, and sweet
As are those orbs of bliss shall be
Our hearts and lips that melting meet.

At last we'll reach you silent isle,
So calm and green amidst the waves,—
So peaceful, too, it does not spurn
The friendly tide its shore that laves.

We'll draw our vessel on the sand,
And seek the shadow of those trees,
Where all alone and undisturbed,
We'll talk and love as we may please.

And then thy voice will be so soft
'T will match the whisper of the leaves,
And then thy breast shall yield its sigh
So like the wavelet as it heaves!

And oh! That eye so dark and free,
So like a spirit in itself!
And then that hand so sweetly small
It would not shame the loveliest elf!

The world might perish all for me,
So that it left that little isle;
The human race might pass away,
If thou remainedst with thy smile.

Then haste, mine own dear Indian maid,
My boat is waiting on its oar;
We'll float upon the tide, my love,
And gaily reach that islet's shore.

www.ingramcontent.com/pod-product-compliance
Lightning Source LLC
LaVergne TN
LVHW052254070426
835507LV00035B/2897